INTIMATE RITUALS AND PERSONAL DEVOTIONS

Spiritual Art through the Ages

Larry David Perkins

with contributions from
Michael Bennett
Oleg Grabar
Robin Poynor
Hulleah J. Tsinhnahjinnie
Dorothy C. Wong

Samuel P. Harn Museum of Art
University of Florida
Gainesville, Florida

THE SAMUEL P. HARN MEMORIAL EXHIBITION

Acknowledgments Inez S. Wolins	1
Intimate Rituals and Personal Devotions **Spiritual Art through the Ages** Larry David Perkins	3
Spiritual Art in Antiquity Michael Bennett	15
Personal Devotional Objects in Buddhist Asia Dorothy C. Wong	23
The Arts of Personal Devotion in African Religion Robin Poynor	37
Most Hesitation Is Not Without History Hulleah J. Tsinhnahjinnie	55
Ritual Objects and Private Devotion **A Random Meditation** Oleg Grabar	65
Selected Bibliography	71
Checklist	73
Photography Credits	78

ACKNOWLEDGMENTS

Innovation is accomplished in art museum exhibitions when a team of curator and staff envisions a change from the usual or offers visitors a new perspective on a body of research. Fresh ideas are presented in challenging ways by identifying and grouping objects differently and by interpreting them so as to provoke and stimulate. The idea of developing an exhibition on the subject of personal spirituality and devotion, drawn from the strength of the Harn Museum of Art's collections, was conceived by Director Emeritus Budd Harris Bishop. Credit for its execution belongs to Larry David Perkins, the Harn Museum's curator of non-western art, who oversaw myriad details to bring this project to fruition. His reflective approach to the study and installation of cross-cultural and multi-cultural objects is groundbreaking for this institution. We are extremely proud of the exhibition and this publication, both of which are a testimony to connoisseurship.

Many individuals contributed to this project. We thank our lenders for their generous support. Their names are listed in this publication in honor of their commitment to the exhibition. We express our gratitude to the guest scholars and advisory committee members who made this project possible. Michael Bennett, Oleg Grabar, Larry David Perkins, Robin Poynor, Hulleah Tsinhnahjinnie, and Dorothy Wong contributed moving essays intended to illuminate the objects in the exhibition and to broaden scholarship.

University of Florida faculty and students were instrumental as well. Our appreciation is extended to professors Aida Bamia, Vasudha Narayanan, and David Stanley for their counsel on the Islamic, Hindu, and Christian sections of the exhibition. Graduate students James Barham, Jamie Johnson, Prita Meier, and Sheena Watson researched objects and wrote label copy.

We are indebted to Rabbi Allan Lehmann of Gainesville and to Rabbi Jerry Schwarzbard of the Library of the Jewish Theological Seminary, New York, for their clarification and educational insights, and to Catherine Simon, curator of the Leon Levy and Shelby White Collection, for her invaluable assistance in securing the loan of Mediterranean antiquities.

Of course, the entire Harn Museum staff made this project a reality. Our thanks are extended to Budd Harris Bishop for his support and encouragement from the onset and to former curator Tom Larose for his work on the Native American selections. Larry David Perkins and I extend special recognition to curatorial assistant Claire Orologas, whose diligent work was vital to the success of the exhibition and catalogue. Her personal devotion and dedication cannot be overstated.

With warm thanks for their many years of discourse and support, we especially acknowledge Dr. David and Mary Ann Cofrin, and the Cofrin family, whose AEC Charitable Trust made this project possible. By honoring Samuel Peebles Harn (1893-1957), a man whose life was committed to his family, to his community, and to service above self, we hope that this first memorial exhibition in the museum that bears his name is an appropriate tribute to his life.

Inez S. Wolins
Director
Samuel P. Harn Museum of Art

Figure 1
Rafael Aragón
American (c. 1796-1862)
Our Lady of Guadalupe
c. 1830s
wood, polychromy
Collections of the Museum of International Folk Art, a unit of the Museum of New Mexico, Santa Fe, bequest of Charles D. Carroll

INTIMATE RITUALS AND PERSONAL DEVOTIONS

Spiritual Art through the Ages

PEOPLE HAVE FASHIONED OBJECTS, IMAGES, AND SACRED SPACES OF SPIRITUAL SIGNIFICANCE ACROSS TIME AND PLACE. THE EARTH STRUCTURES, ROCK PAINTINGS, AND CARVINGS OF PREHISTORY ARE THOUGHT TO REPRESENT EFFORTS TO INFLUENCE THE FORCES OF NATURE, SECURE A SUCCESSFUL HUNT, SEEK PROTECTION FROM ONE'S ENEMIES, INSURE FERTILITY, GIVE THANKS, HONOR OTHER BEINGS, OR PREPARE A PLACE FOR THE AFTERLIFE.

Perhaps we recognize these spiritual intentions as such because they continue to be concerns and motivations shared by religious people to the present day. Similarly, we can easily imagine that these ancient objects, images, and sacred spaces were only a part of a larger ritual context that could also include various botanical and animal offerings, music and dance, and other forms of prescribed behavior. In other words, things fashioned for a spiritual purpose have always obtained their meaning from the context for which they were made and used.

Our recognition of the spiritual significance of objects may be diminished when they are removed from their contexts. This loss may be magnified when we elevate religious objects to the aesthetic realm. Nevertheless, the spiritual significance of religious art is not lost to the devout, nor should our aesthetic appreciation of religious art be diminished by knowledge of its spiritual meaning.

Spiritual art takes many forms. It includes the architecture of sacred places—temples, shrines, *stupas*, churches, cathedrals, synagogues, and mosques—the carvings, paintings, and embellishments that adorn such structures, and the liturgical objects used in them. Given their physical scale and inherently public nature, these may be the most obvious forms of religious art.

Alongside these, however, are other forms of spiritual art, no less ubiquitous, but perhaps less evident given their relatively small scale and use in more private settings. **Intimate Rituals and Personal Devotions: Spiritual Art through the Ages** considers the spiritual meaning and context of such works of art. Some objects in this exhibition served to focus the believer's veneration. Others were an outward expression of spiritual identity. Works of spiritual art may be used by individuals or they may be shared by the family in private settings. Some may relate to personal devotional practices such as pilgrimage, a devotional act common to many parts of the world. This may include the tradition of depositing votive offerings in sacred settings.

The exhibition is meant to make evident that worldwide, works of art have always been created to assist the individual in personal spiritual practice. Thus, **Intimate Rituals and Personal Devotions: Spiritual Art through the Ages** is culturally and historically diverse. Antiquity is represented by works from the ancient Mediterranean world, the earliest more than four-thousand years old. The three monotheistic world religions that originated in the Middle East—Judaism, Christianity, and Islam—are represented with works that range in date from the fourth century to the present. Similarly, Hinduism and Buddhism—two world religions that emerged from India—are featured with works from the fifth century to the present. The indigenous religious traditions of the immense continent of Africa are represented by works from the modern era that may only hint at the rich diversity of ancient traditions so little understood today. Similarly, the spiritual traditions of the Native peoples of the Americas are alluded to by a group of North American works dating largely from the late nineteenth to the early twentieth century.

Spiritual art of a personal nature has been created in many forms. Some—icons, reliquaries, manuscripts, and printed books—may have been intended for public places as well as more intimate settings. Icons made for personal devotion, whether sculptures or paintings, are often smaller versions of those created for public places of worship. Others may make a public appearance only on important occasions, after which they are returned to a private space where they may continue to receive daily devotion. Although manuscripts and printed books are commonly found in public places of worship and serve important liturgical functions there, some types of manuscripts and printed books are by definition personal objects; the book of hours (plate 1) and the illustrated family bible are two such examples. In the Islamic and Buddhist traditions the very making of sacred texts is considered an act of devotion. Other forms—votive offerings, certain commemorative objects, and pilgrimage items—permeate the public/private realms but nevertheless are inherently associated with an individual. Home altars, amulets, pendants, prayer beads, and certain items of clothing are, almost by definition, private forms of devotional art. These forms and the devotional practices they represent appear across cultural, religious, and historical boundaries and underscore the universality of spiritual expression.

HOME ALTARS, SHRINES, AND FAMILY OBSERVANCES

It is not surprising that much of what may be termed intimate ritual and personal devotion takes place in the home. Home altars and shrines may pertain to an individual or be shared by family members. They may be more or less permanent or installed only on special occasions. Permanent altars and shrines may receive the daily attentions of the devout, allowing the integration of spiritual and daily domestic life. They provide the opportunity for constant contact between the devout and the deity. In addition to altars and shrines, many ritually significant and devotional objects may be kept in the home for spiritual observance that may occur daily, at prescribed times, or on special occasions. Several forms of home altars and shrines are mentioned in the essays that follow. Michael Bennett describes a domestic shrine from ancient Egypt. Robin Poynor, writing on the indigenous African works in the exhibition, discusses various types of home altars and shrines that pertain to the individual, the family, and the ancestors. Dorothy Wong explores a number of devotional objects that may be found on Buddhist home altars. Many of the icons, reliquaries, pilgrimage objects, prayer beads, and other objects that are included in the exhibition may at one time have been kept on a home altar or shrine.

There is a rich tradition of home altars in the domestic life of the Hispanic Americas. Elaborate or relatively simple, these altars might include offerings of flowers, incense, votive candles, *ex-votos*, and personal family items. Each altar would be unique, reflecting the particular needs, interests, and devotional focus of the maker. The constructions, in

Figure 2 (left)
José Benito Ortega
American, New Mexico (1858-1941)
Our Lady of Sorrows
before 1907
wood, polychromy, seeds, wire, aluminum
Harn Museum of Art Collection
Gift of Mr. and Mrs. Thomas J. Needham

Figure 3 (right)
St. Vincent Ferrer
Philippines
probably 19th century
wood, polychromy
International Folk Art Foundation Collections
in the Museum of International Folk Art,
a unit of the Museum of New Mexico, Santa Fe

fact, may be considered a form of artistic expression. The heart of Hispanic home altars have been the *santos*, sculpted or painted images of saints or other holy figures such as the Virgin Mary and Christ. Here they would receive daily veneration from family members. *Santos* may take the form of *bultos* (sculptures) or *retablos* (paintings).

The *retablo* by New Mexican *santero* (a maker of *santos*) Rafael Aragón (ca. 1796-1862) depicts *Our Lady of Guadalupe* (figure 1), one of the most beloved devotional images in Mexico and the southwestern United States. According to tradition, in 1531 the Virgin Mary appeared in Mexico to Juan Diego, an Indian peasant. The site of this holy event became a sacred place to Hispanic and Indian Catholics alike. The Basilica of Our Lady of Guadalupe in Mexico City is still an important pilgrimage destination today. Aragón's *retablo* would not only have served as a focal point for daily veneration of the Virgin Mary, it would also have alluded to this notable pilgrimage site. José Benito Ortega (1858-1941) was a well-known maker of *bultos*. His *Our Lady of Sorrows* (figure 2) shares with Aragón's *retablo* a directness of expression typical of New Mexican Hispanic folk artists. Their creations were made for a local population and represent a unique tradition far removed from the painted, carved, and printed prototypes from Europe and Mexico. Sculptural icons from Puerto Rico (plate 2) and the Philippines (figure 3) attest to the prevalence of the tradition throughout the Catholic world. *Our Lady of Montserrat, Miracle of Hormigueros* by José Negrón reflects the popularity of *santos*-making in Puerto Rico today.

Personal and family altars have long been a focus of Hindu devotional practice, as are those established in temples and outdoor shrines. Whether at temple, shrine, or home, Hindu deities are venerated through the performance of *puja* which, at its core involves ritual prayers and offerings. Although the practice of *puja* varies from place to place in the vast Hindu world, it is the vehicle by which Hindus make direct contact with the deity. In a temple, *puja* is performed by a priest, but in the home it is performed by an individual. Typically, the devotee chooses from the Hindu pantheon that deity which seems most appropriate. Among the most prominent are Vishnu, Shiva, and Devi, or one their many manifestations. A visual form of the deity is placed on the home altar and becomes a receptacle for the divine presence. Through the painted, printed, or sculpted image, direct visual contact is made with the deity.

The exhibition includes several icons that could have been placed on Hindu home altars in India. Their small scale makes them particularly suitable for such an environment. Devi and Krishna (figures 4, 5), an avatar of Vishnu, are represented in human form, and the deity Shiva is embodied in the miniature lingam shrine (figure 6).

Home-based rituals and observances, both personal and family oriented, are central to the Jewish tradition. A rich array of works of art are an integral part of these. Perhaps no single object expresses the presence of the spiritual in the daily home life of the devout Jew more than the *mezuzah*. The *mezuzah* is a small piece of parchment on one side of which is inscribed certain passages from the book of Deuteronomy and on the other the word *Shaddai*, meaning God. The parchment is rolled up and placed in a small case, usually of wood or metal. Through an opening in the case, the word *Shaddai* is visible.

The Hebrew word *mezuzah* means doorpost. The *mezuzah*, inside its case, is affixed to the right side of the front doorpost of the home. Reflecting the contemporary vitality of an ancient tradition is the *mezuzah* with its case designed by Jehuda Wolpert in Jerusalem about 1950 (figure 7). The cut-out inscription on Wolpert's case reads, "Blessed shalt thou be when thou comest, and blessed shalt thou be when thou goest out."

Just as the *mezuzah* is an expression of daily devotion, other objects may be incorporated into the observance of the Jewish Sabbath, which begins at nightfall on Friday and ends at sunset on Saturday. This holy day of rest and spiritual renewal is observed in the home and the synagogue and in its fullest expression has a prescribed order. The exhibition includes several objects, dating to the eighteenth and nineteenth centuries, once used for Sabbath service in central and eastern Europe and in Turkey (figure 8). The pair of silver candlesticks from Warsaw, Poland, held candles that would be lit at the beginning of the Sabbath. The small cast, engraved silver cup from Turkey was used in the *Kiddush* ritual during which a blessing is given over a cup of wine. The turret-shaped spice container was fashioned from silver filigree in central Europe. Such containers held cloves and myrtle leaves and would be used in the *Havdalah*, the closing ceremony of the Sabbath. While familiar forms of cups and candlesticks may be adapted for Sabbath use and

Figure 4 (center)
Krishna as the Dancing Butter Thief
Southern India, Madurai area(?)
c. late 17th century
bronze
Harn Museum of Art Collection
Gift of George P. Bickford

Figure 5 (right)
***Krishna Playing the Flute and Dancing
the Rasamandala with the Milkmaids***
Southern India
17th-18th century
bronze
Asian Art Museum of San Francisco
The Avery Brundage Collection

Figure 6 (left)
Miniature Shrine (Shiva's lingam)
India
17th-18th century
gilt silver
Asian Art Museum of San Francisco
The Avery Brundage Collection

identified as such by some form or special marking, spice containers, such as the one here, are unique to this holy weekly observance.

A variety of special objects are identified with the annual Jewish festival of Passover, a commemoration of the Jews' exodus from ancient Egypt. The Passover celebration begins with a special ceremonial meal, the *seder*, during which the story of the exodus is retold through the reading of a liturgical book, the *Haggadah*. The nineteenth-century glass goblet from Bohemia and the eighteenth-century pewter plate from Germany (plate 3) are identified as Passover implements by their inscriptions and designs. An inscription on the goblet is the introduction of the *Haggadah* and reads, "this is the bread of affliction which our forefathers ate in the land of Egypt." On the base of the cup, an inscription repeats another phrase spoken at the *seder*, "Next Year in Jerusalem." The *Haggadah* in the exhibition was printed in 1712 in Amsterdam. Among its many copperplate engravings is one depicting the order of the *seder* in thirteen vignettes (figure 9). That this *Haggadah* saw service in many Passover *seders* seems movingly evident from the many stains on its pages.

PILGRIMAGE AND PORTABILITY

Many forms of art work intended for devotional and ritual use are closely associated with the home. Others are distinguished by their inherent portability or relationship to pilgrimage. Pendants, medals, prayer beads, amulets, and clothing are among a vast class of personal devotional objects and spiritual aids designed to be worn. Book forms—the book of hours, the Bible, the Koran, prayer books among others—are intrinsically portable objects. Many personal religious objects have been designed specifically for travel. These may be portable versions of objects normally associated with the home or public places of worship. Many religious objects obtain their meaning within the context of pilgrimage, an undertaking of personal devotion that dates from antiquity and is still a common practice throughout the world.

A religious pilgrimage is a journey made to a sacred place. Delphi was an important pilgrimage destination in ancient Greece. Every Muslim tries to make a pilgrimage to Mecca at least once in his or her lifetime. Holy sites in Jerusalem have long been important pilgrimage destinations for Jews, Christians, and Muslims. The cathedral of St. James in Santiago de Compostela, Spain, was the culmination of one of the most important pilgrimage routes in Europe. A pilgrimage, however, may also be a less prescribed venture. Any journey to a site which has spiritual significance to the devotee may be considered a pilgrimage. It need not involve a long trip on foot or beast of burden, lasting weeks, months, or even years, although such pilgrimages are still made today. A pilgrimage can be a short hike or can be made by car, train, plane, or tour bus and take place over a weekend or while on a vacation. The anticipation of the visit and the physical separation from daily routine and surroundings prepare the pilgrim for the experience of the sacred place.

Dorothy Wong's discussion of the Buddhist tradition of placing votive offerings at sacred sites throughout Asia resonates with Michael Bennett's description of dedicatory offerings made at sacred places in the ancient Mediterranean world. Such offerings were often made as part of a pilgrimage. Pilgrimage sites have also been places where religious objects could be acquired and taken away as souvenirs, and these often became devotional objects as well. Oleg Grabar writes of how seemingly ordinary objects may obtain extraordinary significance through association with pilgrimage to holy Islamic sites.

One well-known type of memento is the devotional print that began to be produced in the early fifteenth century in Northern Europe. The widespread manufacture of paper enabled the mass production of images. The woodcut technique made it possible to create hundreds of impressions of the same image. This proliferation meant that printed images could be purchased by those of modest means. Monastic pilgrimage sites became important centers for the production and sale of such prints. Typically, these early prints were simple, straightforward images, printed in a single color and often hand-painted, featuring depictions of Christ, the Virgin Mary, and the saints. Two woodcut prints in the exhibition belong to this printmaking tradition: *The Madonna Between Saints Catherine and Barbara* of 1440-1460 and *Christ on the Cross* of 1485 (plate 4). In both, detail was subordinated to the essential imagery. The

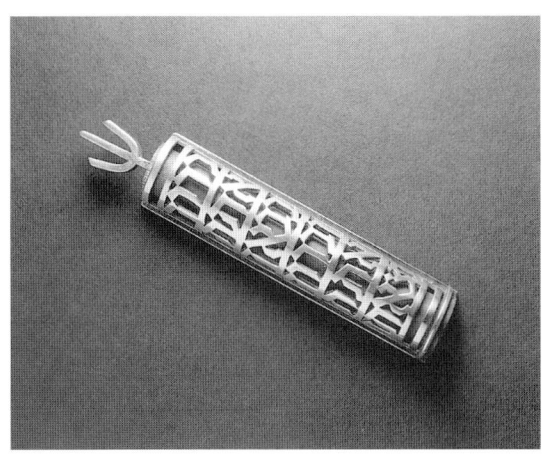

Figure 7
Jehuda Wolpert
American, b. Germany (1900-1981)
Mezuzah and Case
made in Jerusalem, c. 1950
silver, parchment, ink
The Jewish Museum, New York
Gift of Dr. Harry G. Friedman

Figure 8 (left to right)
A. Riedel
Polish
Pair of Sabbath Candlesticks
Warsaw, 1890
silver
The Jewish Museum, New York
Gift in Memory of Bertha Flaxer, presented by her family

Spice Container
Central Europe
late 18th century
silver
The Jewish Museum, New York
Gift of Lucille and Samuel Lemberg

Kiddush Cup with Scroll Handle
Turkey
late 19th century
silver
The Jewish Museum, New York
Gift of Dr. Harry G. Friedman

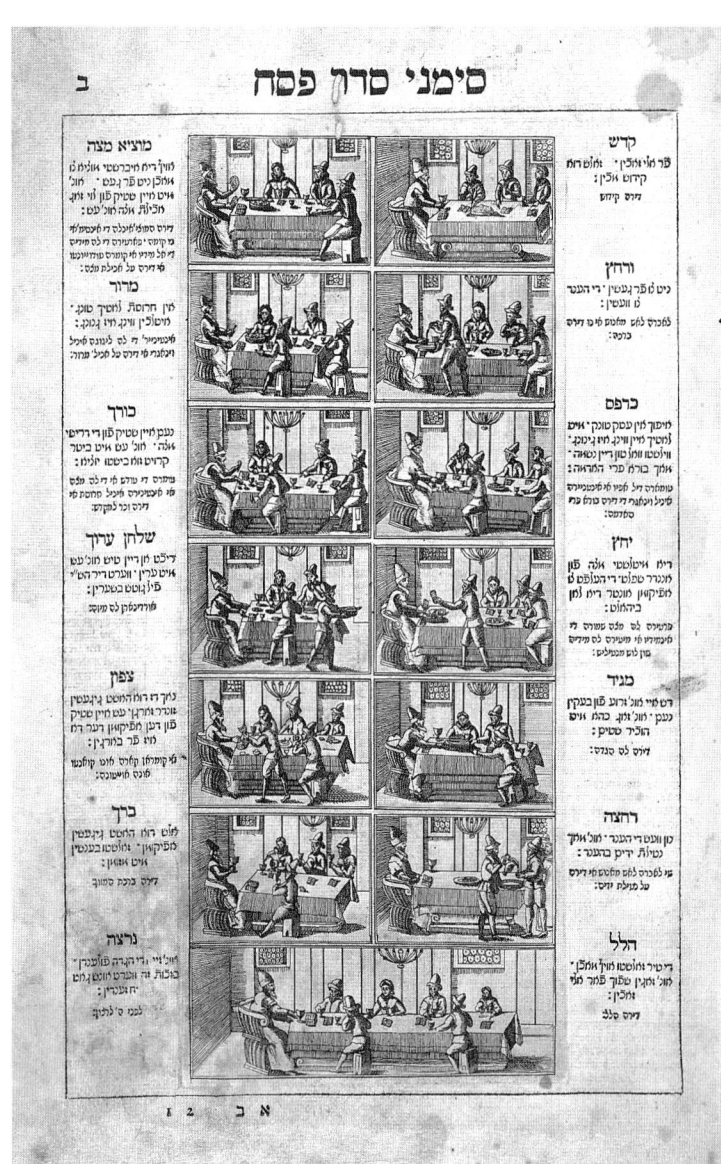

Figure 9
Haggadah
Holland, Amsterdam
1712
black ink on paper with copper-plate engravings
George A. Smathers Libraries, Special Collections and Area Studies

Figure 10
Portable Diptych
Ethiopia
17th century
wood, tempera
Courtesy, Peabody Essex Museum, Salem, MA

Figure 11 (top)
Ga'u
Tibet
18th century
brass, silver, clay, polychromy, cowrie shells, bells, cloth
Harn Museum of Art Collection
Museum purchase, funds provided by museum visitors

Figure 12 (bottom)
Reliquary Cross
Byzantine
10th-12th century
gilt silver
Harn Museum of Art Collection
Museum purchase, gift of Michael A. Singer

purpose was not to tell a story but rather to provide an iconic form to help focus the dovotee's meditation on the holy figures. Prints such as these were obviously valued more as devotional images than as precious works of art, for even given the huge numbers that were produced, relatively few have survived. They have been found pasted onto boxes, tipped into books, and fashioned into portable altars. The vast majority, it seems, were literally used up. It is partly because of their rarity that they are so highly prized today.

The design of many devotional objects made them well-suited for travel. The Gothic crucifixion panel from northern France was once part of a hinged diptych (plate 5). Deeply carved in ivory, in its complete form it could have been folded for travel thereby protecting the delicate imagery within. Also featuring a devotional image of the crucifixion, the Ethiopian diptych would be easily transportable given its small size (figure 10). From the Buddhist tradition, a finely made silver box enshrines an amulet of a Bodhisattva (figure 11). A cord could be strung through the shallow loops on the side of the box, allowing the portable shrine to be attached to the devotee during travel.

Many objects were meant to be worn constantly, perhaps to serve protective functions but also as an expression of spiritual devotion. The Byzantine pectoral cross with an image of Christ on one side and the Virgin on the other is actually a reliquary (figure 12). Whether it still holds the sacred relic originally placed inside it is unknown. Similarly, a silver and amber neck piece was once worn as an amulet by a Somali Muslim woman (plate 6). The silver tube would have contained (and may still) an inscription from the Koran.

That ritual and devotional objects such as these are no longer being used in their contexts or serving the functions for which they were made calls into question their present-day spiritual viability. The questioning becomes especially acute when the objects under consideration were made for personal and private use and are being collected and placed on public display in a decidedly secular institution. There can be no doubt that the original significance of a spiritual work of art at least changes when it is no longer a part of its original context. It cannot be categorically stated, however, that religious objects lose all spiritual significance when they are collected or placed on public display. That determination must remain the prerogative of the religious individual, whose response to the public display of spiritual art will be varied and unpredictable. Perhaps it is in the nature of things that meaning can change. Both Hulleah Tsinhnahjinnie and Oleg Grabar address these issues in their insightful essays. But if religious works of art remain spiritually viable in the museum context, what, if any, responsibility does the institution have to accommodate the devout visitor?

Related to the question of context and meaning is that we cannot know for certain that every work of art presented in this exhibition ever served a spiritual purpose; it is, in fact, likely that some were acquired by their original owners as works of art or objects of curiosity. Provenance indicates, however, that many were at one time objects of intimate ritual or personal devotion, and that some, on loan from private collections, still are. For many, stains, scars, tears, burns, smoke, patina, and the loss of surfaces and features through endless touching and countless rubbings provide moving testimony of their use as spiritual objects.

Finally, although we have endeavored to give breadth to the exhibition by including examples from numerous cultures and traditions, many parts of the world and many spiritual traditions could not be represented; the field is too vast. We hope that the diversity presented here will provide some sense of the richness and variety of spiritual works of art that have been created for personal devotion and intimate ritual.

Larry David Perkins
Curator of Non-Western Art
Samuel P. Harn Museum of Art

Figure 13
Statuette of a Standing Worshiper
Mesopotamia or Syria
c. 2400 B.C.E.
limestone
Lent by Shelby White and Leon Levy

SPIRITUAL ART IN ANTIQUITY

IN ANTIQUITY, AS TODAY, RELIGION WAS VITAL FOR GIVING MEANING TO THE MYSTERIOUS EXPERIENCES OF LIFE.

We would, for example, recognize the ancient conviction that the divine was implicit in the mystery of birth and death, in the miracle of answered prayers, or in heavenly interventions. Yet even the most devout among us would not view "religion" in remotely the same ways as did the ancient Mesopotamians, Egyptians, Greeks, or Romans. A pervasive objectivity separates us from ancient religious ideas and practices. It is now common for spiritual or religious concerns to co-exist with scientific standards of proof. We routinely isolate the secular from the religious, as in the "separation of church and state," and place matters of faith on a different plane from those of reason. For much of antiquity, this way of thinking doubtless would have seemed very strange and even incomprehensible.

Before Greek Ionian philosophy of the sixth century B.C.E., it would have been difficult to detect a difference between objective and subjective, as all explanations of empirical phenomena were expressed poetically in the form of myth. Both the Mesopotamians and the Egyptians understood natural events as expressions of divine will, not as impersonal laws of physics subject to verification through detached calculation and experimentation. A correlate of this way of apprehending the world is a tendency to merge what we might consider a symbol with its object. For the ancients, an object may have been imbued with an utterly tangible reality easily missed by a modern viewer. Consequently, abstractions such as "life" and "death" may be given the weight of concrete objects. From this perspective, a "ritual" act may be equivalent to the act itself and a dream may have the same meaning as an experience while awake. This profoundly personal relationship between mankind, nature, and the divine is important for modern viewers to bear in mind when looking at ancient objects of spiritual significance.

The art objects in this section of the exhibition range in date from the third millennium B.C.E. to the fifth century C.E. They are Mesopotamian, Minoan, Egyptian, Greek (mainland, Cretan, and probably from Magna Graecia), and Roman. As a group, they represent an excellent sample of devotional, commemorative, and dedicatory works of very high aesthetic merit. Each embodies a distinctive spiritual sensibility deriving from its function, culture, and context. The depth and quality of the group make practical a chronological discussion, taking each object in turn.

Mankind's position was precarious within the Mesopotamian cosmos. Natural forces—floods, droughts, pestilence, and plague—were recognized as dangerous divinities. Major gods accorded with cosmological spheres. For example, An (Anu), father of the gods, was responsible for the upper atmosphere. His son Enlil occupied the air between heaven and earth, and so controlled the weather. Fear of the malevolent temper of gods such as Enlil permeates Mesopotamian religious observance. Because each of the manifold aspects of nature had a willful personality, it was crucial to know these gods and to gain their favor if at all possible. Just as the sun warmed the crops and the rain fed them, the gods spread benevolence in a world in which the dynasty in heaven reflected the social order on earth.

The well-preserved Mesopotamian or Syrian limestone statuette of a standing bearded man with shaved head wearing a tufted skirt certainly represents a worshiper transfixed by a divine presence (figure 13). With his hands clasped in front, his once inlaid eyes stared in awe at the cult statue of a god in a temple. Dated to the mid-third-millennium B.C.E. (Early Dynastic Period), such statuettes were sometimes inscribed with the names of their donors in addition to a message or prayer. The donor's life essence was somehow considered to reside in the statuette, held in a posture of tireless and hopeful devotion.

In Minoan Crete, encounters with divinity usually occurred out-of-doors, perhaps near a sacred pillar or tree, in a cave, or before a special architectural façade. Minoan gods and goddesses did not seem to require houses as did Mesopotamian deities, but clear indications of their power may be seen in statuettes of worshipers who either anticipate or actually sense their presence. In Minoan art, more emphasis is placed on the human reaction to the epiphany of a god than on the actual appearance of the god. Dancing, sacrifice, or prayer could induce the divinity to commune with mortals. The exquisite Minoan bronze statuette of a woman, dated to the middle of the second millennium B.C.E. (figure 14), holds its right hand to its forehead, a gesture also common to statuettes of men. The figure wears the Minoan flared skirt with a swath of material around the waist. Her arms are sleeved and her breasts exposed in the Minoan fashion. The pose may signal adoration or some other emotional state. Behind this statuette was a religious ecstasy now unfortunately lost to us.

The deified Egyptian pharaoh was the isolated single intermediary between gods and humans. The son of the supreme god, Amun-Re, the pharaoh alone was responsible for building temples and acting as the highest of priests in ceremonies with the gods. On these occasions, he was negotiating with his own kind for the benefit of mankind. The pharaoh was the shepherd of his people. One of the visible emblems of his office was the *heqa*-scepter, or shepherd's crook, which also stood for the word "to rule" in the Egyptian language. In association with the pharaoh, the gods made life itself possible. They controlled all natural forces and seasonal rhythms, the waters of the Nile, the cooling winds. They regulated the celestial bodies that set in motion and calibrated the passage of time. The Egyptians gave thanks to pharaoh for all life-giving things that sustained and insured their existence.

The Egyptian veneration of the deified pharaoh is vividly and eloquently illustrated by the painted limestone domestic shrine made during the reign of Tuthmosis III, Dynasty 18 (figure 15). The shrine resembles the doorway of a temple with the wooden doors now missing. These would have been opened to reveal the image of a round-topped stele set back in a door frame. Inscriptions identify the seated pharaoh on the stele as Tuthmosis III, and the owner of the shrine who commissioned it as Amenemheb, a *sedjem-ash* (cemetery worker/craftsman). Tuthmosis III is shown seated on a throne under a winged sun disk and holding a *heqa*-scepter (shepherd's crook) and *ankh*-sign (sign of life). He wears the Blue Crown with uraeus (protective divine serpent associated with kingship) and bull's tail, signs of his supreme office and supernatural status. On a table before him are abundant offerings of food and flowers. With the aid of this shrine, probably displayed in his home, Amenemheb could privately venerate the god-king, source of all prosperity, goodness, and justice on earth.

The Greek Olympian deities, presided over by Zeus, are already fully articulated in Homeric poetry. By the eighth century B.C.E. these poems, the product of a long tradition of oral composition reaching back to the Bronze Age, attained monumental proportions in the *Iliad* and the *Odyssey*, great epics that appealed to pan-Hellenic audiences. Newly established pan-Hellenic sanctuaries such as those of Olympia and Delphi attest to the increasing importance of the *polis* (city-state) over the older family-based political structures (*oikos, genos*). Greek sanctuaries and Homeric poetry represent the common identity shared by Greeks no matter their *polis* affiliations. The sanctuaries were places where Greeks gathered to worship gods and goddesses, consult oracles, attend various poetry and musical performances, and compete in or watch athletic competitions such as the Olympic games (established in 776 B.C.E.). The Greek *polis* was the setting for monumental temples devoted to patron deities, sometimes located in an elevated

Figure 15 (center)
Domestic Shrine
Egypt, Thebes
New Kingdom, Dynasty 18
Reign of Tuthmosis III (c. 1479-1425 B.C.E.)
limestone
The Cleveland Museum of Art
Gift of the John Huntington Art and
Polytechnic Trust

Figure 14 (left)
Female Statuette
Crete, Minoan
c. 1600-1450 B.C.E.
bronze
Courtesy of the Arthur M. Sackler Museum
Harvard University Art Museums
David M. Robinson Fund and Gift of Mr. and
Mrs. Edwin L. Weisl, Jr.

Figure 16 (right)
Ram Bearer (Kriophoros)
Greece, Crete
7th century B.C.E.
terra cotta, polychromy
The Cleveland Museum of Art
John L. Severance Fund

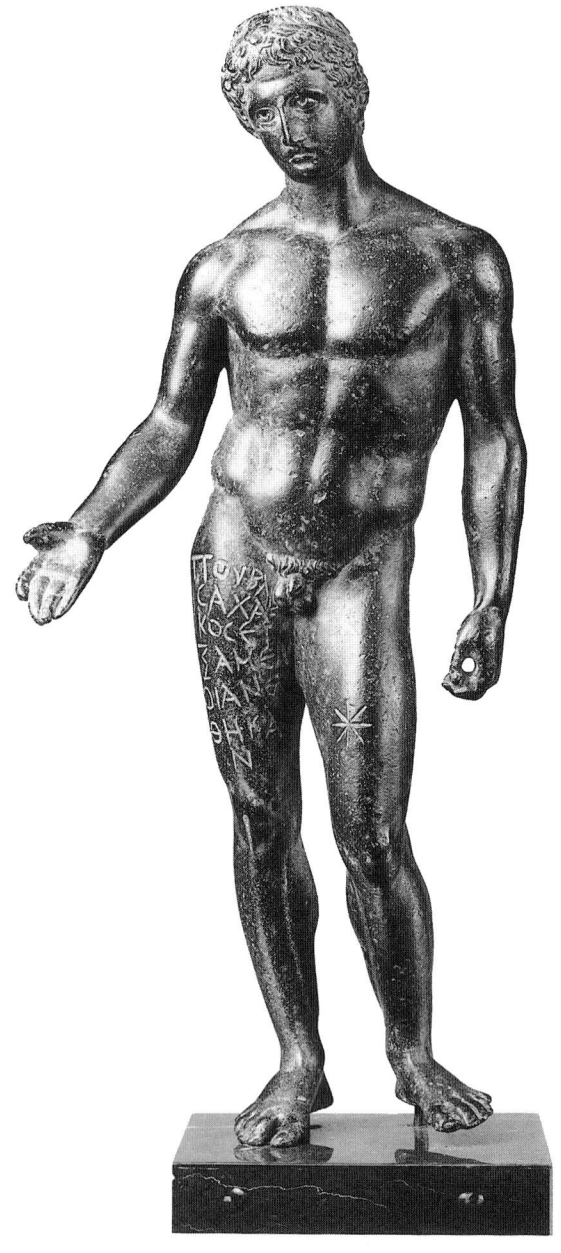

Figure 17 (left)
Statuette of a Nude Youth (Kouros)
Probably from Magna Graecia
Archaic, c. 480-470 B.C.E.
bronze, copper
Lent by Shelby White and Leon Levy

Figure 18 (right)
Statuette of a Worshiper
Roman, Early Imperial
1st half of the 1st century C.E.
bronze, silver
Inscribed on the right leg: ΠΟΥΒΛΙΣ ΑΧΑΕΙΚΟΣ ΕΙΞΑΜΕΝΟΙ
ΑΝΕΘΗΚΑΝ: "Publi[o]s Achaiikos, having vowed, dedicated [this]."
Lent by Shelby White and Leon Levy

religious/civic center, as in the acropolis ("high-city") of Athens. The invention of the Greek alphabet, adapted from the Phoenician alphabet to the sounds of the Greek language in the eighth century B.C.E., ushered in the beginning of Greek literature. This was a time of intellectual renaissance in the arts, in politics, and in religion.

The art of eighth century B.C.E. Greece, called "Geometric," displays a spare and elegant sense of design. Natural forms are reduced to refined fundamentals. A limited number of abstract and representational motifs are combined in vast and complex painted decorative compositions on the surfaces of large fired clay vases. One of the earliest and most characteristic images of Greek Geometric art was the horse. Horses are ubiquitous in the art of the period, painted on vases, sculpted in clay, and cast in bronze. Surely the horse conveyed aristocratic and elite associations, since raising the animals, then as now, required considerable means. Beyond expressions of wealth and status, the horse was also appreciated for its impressive physical beauty, strength, and grace.

Judged by its size, formal proportions, or state of preservation, the stately eighth century B.C.E. cast bronze horse (plate 7) is one of the very finest produced by a Corinthian workshop. Likely dedicated at a sanctuary to a god or goddess, the statuette distills the horse's silhouette to a minimum of perfectly balanced component parts. Emphasis is placed on the tall stately neck, the front and rear haunches, and the flaring muzzle connected to forward pointing ears. The openwork base of alternating triangular-shaped apertures may represent the transparency of water, a pool or a stream. Surface embellishment includes concentric circles and zigzags, visible on both sides of the neck. Its profile is a study of delicate balance and bold conception, iconic of its period and culture. Horse rearing was an aristocratic preoccupation in early Greece. This statuette was both a gift to the gods and a sign of elite status.

Greek colonization, both east to the western coast of Asia Minor and west to south Italy and Sicily in the eighth century B.C.E., brought Greeks into contact with several other cultures, some of great antiquity and sophistication. Euboean Greeks established a trading center at Al Mina in northern Syria in the ninth century B.C.E. Greek contacts in the east, the interaction with eastern craftsmen who traveled to Greece (notably to Crete), and the importation of eastern works of art into Greece, all contributed to a dramatic change in Greek art in the seventh century B.C.E. Art historians and archaeologists therefore call this period "Orientalizing."

The striking painted terra cotta statuette (figure 16) of a warrior with a ram across his shoulders (*kriophoros*) dates to this dynamic period of cultural transition. It is one of the most important and powerful Greek seventh century B.C.E. terra cottas to have survived. Designed as a half-length figure, its body is hollow, and an added clay shim at the back suggests that it was once part of a larger assemblage. Perhaps it had been a vessel protome or part of a temple model or pedimental group. The color and texture of the fired clay and painted slip are at home on Crete. The strict frontality of the figure, with its triangular-shaped face and stiff wig-like hair, associates it with other seventh-century "Daedalic"-style sculptures. The term is taken from the legendary Athenian craftsman and sculptor Daedalus, who was credited with designing the famous labyrinth at Knossos on Crete for King Minos. Mold-made Near Eastern terra cottas may have been the inspiration for the style, seen also in larger works in stone.

The seventh century B.C.E. terra cotta *kriophoros*, one of the earliest such figures known, is thus far unique in representing a warrior. The few other sculptures of this type are shepherds and, later, the god Hermes. The figure wears the panoply of a Homeric hero: a cap-like helmet, breastplates, and heroic waist belt (*zoster*). The *Iliad* and the *Odyssey* both use the *zoster* as an attribute of heroic power and status. The archaic *hoplite* warrior, by contrast, wore the bronze bell-corslet. The iconography of the *kriophoros* may have been inspired by north Syrian stone reliefs showing offering bearers in the same pose. This pose would have a very long history, becoming, in the Christian era, the image of "the good shepherd." The Cretan terra cotta imparts a heroic ambiance to a ritual act of sacrifice, linking the hero to the divine.

Those Greeks who immigrated west in the eighth century B.C.E. retained their culture in what came to be known as "Great Greece" (*Magna Graecia*). By the Classical period, the coasts of southern Italy and Sicily were dotted with Greek city-states, all producing works of art in the Greek style. As on the Greek mainland, art commonly served a religious function as dedications to divinities at temples or within sanctuaries. The dedication may have been an offering of thanks or a gift to inspire a divine favor. These offerings could take the form of statuettes, themselves sometimes reflecting famous large-scale masterpieces.

The forceful bronze *kouros* ("young man"), probably the work of a western Greek sculptor, may have been a dedicatory offering (figure 17). Dated between 480 and 470 B.C.E., the large statuette of an athletic youth may once have held a *phiale* in its missing right hand for libation to the gods. In the manner of large marble *kouroi*, the left leg steps forward of the right. The hair is rolled under a fillet at the back of the head and is cut short with small curls above the eyebrows. Anatomical details are executed with great care. The nipples are inlaid in copper. The sharply defined facial features display an alert expression. The body musculature is well-articulated. This is especially notable in the torso: the pectorals, the abdominal region, and the upper shoulders. Forever youthful and beautiful, the statuette may once have offered a silent prayer, now forgotten.

Bronze dedicatory statuettes in Greek style continued to be produced into Roman times. The inscribed statuette, dated from 1 to 40 C.E., is clearly in the tradition of Polyclitus, the famous Greek Argive sculptor of the mid-fifth century B.C.E. (figure 18). Its open right hand probably once held a *phiale* and its left perhaps an *oinochoe* (wine pitcher). The large silver inlaid eyes look up while the head is tilted down. The fillet around the head is tied at the front. This detail, together with its nudity, suggests an athlete. The inscription cut into the right thigh of the statuette after casting contains misspellings, but it may be translated thus, "Publi[o]s Achaiikos, having vowed, dedicated [this]." An eight-pointed star was incised on the left thigh presumably at the same time. With its classical *contrapposto* and reference to a Polyclitan original, the statuette combines a Roman votive function with a Greek ideal of human perfection.

For many Romans, the rituals of death and burial called for commemoration of the deceased through portraiture. In a remarkable series of marble funerary sculptures, the members of the family of Vibia Drosis are remembered in portraits stylistically consistent with the various times of their deaths. Vibia Drosis commissioned three stelai between 69 and 80 C.E. All share the same essential features: tall rectangular shaft with portrait niche at the top and a loculus with inscription below. An inscription identifies one stele as belonging to Gaius Vibius Felix, Vibia Drosis's father, whose portrait reflects a hairstyle current in the Julio Claudian period (figure 19). He died at age 49. According to another inscription, her son, Gaius Vibius Severus, lived only 23 years. His portrait shows a whiskered young man with a hairstyle popular during the reign of Nero (figure 20). Vibia Drosis's own stele records that she made it, "for herself and her descendants" (figure 21). Her Flavian period coiffure of corkscrew curls shows that she outlived her son. Sometime between 85 and 95 C.E., Vibia Drosis also commissioned the modest cinerary urn of Gaius Vibius Herostratus (figure 22). This wonderful group of funerary sculptures documents one Roman woman's successful attempt to preserve, in words and images, the memory of her family.

Borrowed from Egypt and assimilated first by the Greeks in the Hellenistic period and then by the Romans, the goddess Isis became a divinity of universal power in later antiquity. In the late Roman Empire, Isis was worshiped for her life-bestowing powers, including a connection with life after death. The mold-made terra cotta statuette of *Isis Lactans* (not pictured) was excavated from a tomb at Beth Shean in Palestine and dates from the fourth to fifth century C.E. (figure 32). Isis, hair braided and nude from the waist up, offers her breast to an infant, either the god Harpocrates or Horus. The later image of the *Virgin Lactans* (Virgin Mary) was derived from representations of Isis, demonstrating a continuity of religious iconography from pagan to Christian.

Michael Bennett
Associate Curator of Greek and Roman Art
Cleveland Museum of Art

Figure 19 (left)
Stele of Gaius Vibius Felix
Roman, Early Flavian
c. 69-80
marble
Lent by Shelby White and Leon Levy

Figure 20 (center)
Stele of Gaius Vibius Severus
Roman, Early Flavian
c. 69-80
marble
Lent by Shelby White and Leon Levy

Figure 21 (right)
Stele of Vibia Drosis
Roman, Early Flavian
c. 69-80
marble
Lent by Shelby White and Leon Levy

Figure 22 (bottom left)
Cinerary Urn of Gaius Vibius Herostratus
Roman, Early Flavian
c. 85-95
marble
Lent by Shelby White and Leon Levy

Figure 23
***Digambara Jaina Shrine of the
Tirthankara Rsabanatha***
India, Northern Karnatika, Kolhapur(?),
Chalukya(?)
c. 11th or 12th century
bronze
Harn Museum of Art Collection
Gift of George P. Bickford

PERSONAL DEVOTIONAL OBJECTS

in Buddhist Asia

BUDDHISM IS A UNIVERSAL RELIGION THAT HAS INFLUENCED THE DEVELOPMENTS OF MOST ASIAN CIVILIZATIONS. THE RELIGION WAS FOUNDED BY SIDDHARTHA GAUTAMA (563-483 B.C.E.), WHO WAS BORN A PRINCE OF THE SHAKYA PEOPLE IN A KINGDOM IN THE FOOTHILLS OF PRESENT-DAY NEPAL. SIDDHARTHA WAS BROUGHT UP IN SHELTERED LUXURY IN THE PALACE, BUT WHEN HE BECAME AWARE OF THE SUFFERINGS OF LIFE HE LEFT THE PALACE IN SEARCH OF ANSWERS TO LIFE'S EXISTENTIAL QUESTIONS.

At first he became an ascetic in the forest; however, he realized that extreme asceticism was not the answer, but that the Middle Way, a path of balance, was the way to enlightenment. When Gautama gained understanding of the ultimate truth, he became known as the Buddha, "the Awakened One." He was also given the honorific title of Shakyamuni, or "sage of the Shakya clan." Among the Buddha's many teachings are the Four Noble Truths, which hold that life is full of suffering; the cause of suffering is desire; the means to end the suffering caused by the chain of birth and rebirth (*samsara*) is to eliminate desire; and enlightenment may be gained by following an eightfold path which emphasizes moral discipline. Having gained this insight at the age of thirty-five, the Buddha spent the rest of his life traveling and teaching. He established the monastic order (the *sangha*) for his followers, advocating the ideal of the monk. When he passed away, the Buddha was said to have attained Nirvana, total extinction or the end of the cycle of birth and rebirth. The Buddha, the Dharma (his teachings), and the *sangha* came to be known as the Three Treasures of the religion.

Buddhism continued to grow after the Buddha's death. By the time of the common era, a schism occurred within the religion, dividing the early schools, called Hinayana (the small vehicle), from the later schools, called Mahayana (the great vehicle). The older schools of Buddhism emphasized morality and spiritual discipline as a path to personal salvation. In the new schools, however, the emphasis shifted to devotional faith and reliance on the supernatural powers of the Buddha and other deities for salvation.

The growth of Mahayana Buddhism in the first few centuries of the common era also witnessed the interactions with and mutual influences of Buddhism and the other two Indian religions, Hinduism and Jainism. The rise of the Mahayana cults of Bodhisattvas—spiritual beings who were destined to gain enlightenment but postponed it for the benefit of suffering beings—for example, coincided with the developments of theistic worship of Hindu gods such as Shiva, Vishnu, and Devi (the Great Goddess); Krishna, an incarnation of Vishnu, later became one of the most popular devotional deities (see figures 4-6). Buddhist and Hindu deities took on iconographic marks and attributes that resembled each other; for example, Avalokiteshvara, the Bodhisattva of Compassion, shared many features with the Hindu god Shiva. Jainism, founded in the sixth century B.C.E., emphasized monasticism and an austere, ascetic code of behavior. Although atheistic, Jains worshiped their prophets called *Tirthankaras*. Images of *Tirthankaras* began to be made about the same time the Buddha began to be represented in anthropomorphic form. Jain and Buddha images also resembled each other, except that the former type were distinguished by their nakedness. Like Buddhist and Hindu icons, *Tirthankaras* were honored in household shrines in personal devotional worship (figure 23).

Originally the Buddha was anchored in the historical person of Gautama. In Mahayana Buddhism the concept of the Buddha became deified and abstracted into a transcendent being. Ultimately the Buddha was identified with his teachings, the Dharma. To express the notion that the Buddha's teachings were eternal and omnipresent, Buddhists believed that numerous Buddhas existed in past, present, and future ages, and in all regions of space. Personifications of the different qualities or epithets of the Buddha gave rise to a large pantheon of colorful characters. Most important of all, Bodhisattvas became major cult figures in devotional Buddhism. Spirits and deities from the Hindu and Indian folk traditions have also been incorporated into the Buddhist pantheon. As a result, later devotional Buddhism was characterized by a large number of deities to whom devotees prayed for intercession, protection, and blessings.

From its origin in India, Buddhism spread to other parts of Asia. Hinayana Buddhism influenced countries in South and Southeast Asia, including Sri Lanka, Burma, and Thailand. Mahayana Buddhism spread to North and East Asia: China, Korea, and Japan. The last stage of the development of Buddhism is called Vajrayana (or Tantrayana) and was practiced primarily in Tibet and, to some extent, in Japan. Vajrayana placed special emphases on ritual, such as the use of *dharani* (short phrases that embody the Buddha's teachings) for magical efficacy, and meditative practices.

Devotional practices in Buddhism are performed on both formalized, regular occasions as well as in more informal, private ways. Regular visits to Buddhist temples to worship, to pray, to learn about the Buddha's teachings, and to make offerings were and still are an important part of devotees' religious activities.

Worshipers may also embark on long and sometimes arduous journeys to visit the holy sites. In India the sacred sites first evolved around locations associated with key events in the Buddha's life. Later, in India and in other Buddhist countries, the list of holy sites enumerated, developing into important pilgrimage routes. During the journey to holy places, pilgrims were physically removed from the routine of their daily lives, anticipating their coming into the presence of divinities in sacred spaces. En route, the participation in devotional practices such as chanting, praying, or meditation heightened their emotive experience of the sacred. If traveling in groups, the atmosphere of piety and devotion was further reinforced with a sense of community.

In early Buddhist India, the Buddha was not represented in anthropomorphic form. Instead, worship focused on *stupas*, mounds that contained the Buddha's relics. Around the first century C.E., coinciding with the development of the Mahayana, anthropomorphic images of the Buddha and Bodhisattvas began to be made. Buddhist temples or rock-cut caves enshrined sculptural or mural depictions of icons as well as narratives for worship and meditation. At Buddhist shrines or pilgrimage sites, worshipers offered incense and flowers. In addition, they made votive offerings of miniature *stupas*, clay tablets, or plaques containing images or Buddhist phrases. They also purchased personal icons, talismans, amulets, and charms to take away as souvenirs. Usually carried on the body, these devotional objects were believed to protect the wearer from evil, illness, or harm. Sometimes a printed record of a pilgrim's map served to remind the individual of the journey and was a testimony to his/her piety (plate 8).

Monastic or lay Buddhists also carried out daily private rituals of devotional worship. They prayed, meditated, and made offerings of flowers and incense to deities to whom they vowed obeisance and from whom they sought blessings and protection. Small sculptural icons were sometimes placed in household shrines and pictorial images were hung on the wall, serving as the focus for devotional worship and meditation. When praying or reciting the names of Buddhist

Figure 24 (left)
Miniature Votive Stupa
China, Gansu Province
Northern Liang Period (397-460)
dated 435
steatite
The Cleveland Museum of Art
Purchase from the J. H. Wade Fund

Figure 25 (center)
Miniature Stupa with Illustrations of Jataka Tales
China
Five Dynasties Period (907-960)
dated 955
bronze
Courtesy of the Arthur M. Sackler Museum
Harvard University Art Museums
Gift of Nasli M. Heeramaneck

Figure 26 (right)
Miniature Pagoda Containing a Printed Dharani Charm
Japan
c. 764-770
wood, gesso
Courtesy, Peabody Essex Museum, Salem, MA

Figure 27 (top center)
Stupa Reliquary
China
Tang Dynasty (618-907)
silvered bronze
Harn Museum of Art Collection
Museum purchase, gift of
Dr. and Mrs. David A. Cofrin
1999.16

Figure 28 (center)
Shakyamuni Preaching: A Votive Stele
China
Northern Zhou Dynasty (557-581)
c. 565
yellow mottled stone
The Cleveland Museum of Art
Gift of the John Huntington Art and Polytechnic Trust

Figure 29 (left)
Shakyamuni
Korea
Koryo Period
(918-1392)
wood, traces of black lacquer
The Cleveland Museum of Art
John L. Severance Fund

Figure 30 (right)
Seated Buddha
Indonesia, Java
9th century
bronze
Asian Art Museum of San Francisco
Gift of the Lyda Ebert Foundation

deities, prayer beads or a gong were used. The Buddha's relics or Buddhist texts sometimes replaced icons as objects of devotional worship.

Common forms of personal devotional objects in Buddhist Asia included votive *stupas* (reliquaries), household shrines, small icons, votive tablets or plaques, talismans, block-printed images and charms, rosaries, and *sutras* (Buddhist sacred texts). Relatively small, they were mostly portable and could be easily carried. Depending on the donor's economic means, some of these objects were exquisite works of art fashioned with sumptuous materials. Others were mass-produced with little concern for artistic quality; what was important was the symbolic significance and the magical efficacy of the objects.

Two major principles guided the creation of devotional objects. First, sacredness and supernatural power were endowed upon certain material objects, which in turn served as objects of devotion. Articles such as relics, *stupas*, icons, tablets, amulets, and sacred texts were deemed sacred because of their associations with either the physical presence or the teachings of the Buddha. They were thought to be repositories of power—the superhuman power of the Buddha and other deities and saints who have gained knowledge of transcendent truth. The transference of magical properties to material objects was manifested in a number of cults in the Buddhist tradition: the cult of relics, the cult of images, the cult of votive tablets and amulets, and the cult of books. In sociological terms, the "charisma" of the Buddha as a religious founder and leader has been objectified and concretized in physical matters. Buddhist institutions manufactured votive objects for sale to worshipers and pilgrims, who donated them as offerings or kept them as souvenirs or personal talismans. In economic terms, the mass production and consumption of votive objects constituted a process of fetishism and commercialization of these objects.

Second, the Buddhist notion of charity (*dana*) as an act of piety and a means of accumulating merit was another motivational force behind the practice of making votive offerings. In Mahayana Buddhism especially, the advocation of making donations as a religious virtue was cultivated to involve the laity. Passages from Buddhist scriptures exhorted worshipers to honor the Buddha or objects that were reminders of the Buddha's presence by making offerings. Worshipers were also urged to give to monks and monasteries, since Buddhist institutions relied on donations from lay followers. In return worshipers gained religious merit for their material gifts. In East Asia, the Buddhist concept of transference of merit merged with funeral cults; donors often made offerings for the benefit of deceased relatives or for rebirth in the Pure Land.

STUPA AND RELIC WORSHIP

One of the earliest forms of Buddhist devotional practice focused on the *stupa*—the mound containing the Buddha's relics. In India there was an ancient tradition of building large funeral mounds to honor kings or great men. After the Buddha's death, his body was cremated and the ashes and remains were divided and placed in relic mounds in different places for followers to worship.

Some of the greatest *stupas* in early Buddhist India have survived from the few centuries before and after the common era, including those at Bharhut and Sanchi in central India and at Amaravati in southern India. The Indian *stupa* consists of a base, a round drum, a hemispherical dome, and a mast with several umbrellas of gradually diminishing sizes. The structure is enclosed within a railing with gates placed at the four cardinal directions. Architecturally the stupa is conceived as a cosmological diagram. The mast, rising from the dome-shaped mound, symbolizes the world tree or axis of the world. The parasol, a symbol of royalty, is an emblem of the Buddha's role as a spiritual ruler of the universe.

Reliquaries and other sacred deposits were placed in a sealed chamber inside the *stupa*. A relic can be hair, ashes, or a tiny fragment of bone. Objects associated with the Buddha, such as fragments of his begging bowl or his robe, are also considered relics. Buried alongside the relics were offerings made by donors—small objects in gold, silver, pearl, precious or semiprecious stones, or glass beads that were once used as rosaries. Reliquaries were fashioned in a variety of shapes, frequently as miniature *stupas* containing all the elements of the large structures.

When visiting a *stupa*, pilgrims pay respect by circumambulating the monument in a clockwise direction. The railing and sometimes the body of the *stupa* are embellished with carvings of Buddhist narratives and other motifs. These carvings serve as visual aids for contemplation, reminding the viewers of the Buddha's path of enlightenment as a model to follow. Pilgrims also make offerings of flowers, incense, and votive items, which they purchase at the *stupa* sites or nearby monasteries and which they sometimes take away as mementoes.

Lay worshipers contributed towards the building of *stupas*. Passages from canonical Buddhist texts encouraged worshipers to build *stupas* to honor the Buddha. Such devotional acts would generate merit, for builders, donors, and worshipers. It did not matter what size the *stupas* were. Many pilgrims dedicated miniature reliquaries as offerings, large numbers of which have been found in and around *stupa* and monastery sites in India. Votive *stupas* were fashioned in a variety of materials. Modest examples made of clay were pressed from molds and then baked or sun-dried. Like votive plaques or tablets (see discussion below), these terra cotta *stupas* were mass-produced and were among the most common forms of devotional offerings. Some of these *stupas* contained an impression of the Buddhist creed— a phrase or sentence that represents the Buddha's words or teachings. Placing miniature *stupas* bearing the Buddha's words functioned to consecrate the holy sites. The hair or ashes of eminent Buddhist monks or saints were sometimes mixed with the clay for fashioning these *stupas* as well as other votive objects.

As Buddhism spread to other parts of Asia, the *stupa* took a variety of forms: from the multistoried *pagoda* of East Asia, the *dagoba* of Nepal and Tibet, to the grand expression of the *stupa* as a three-dimensional cosmic diagram at Borobudur, Java. Because of the diversification in form, votive *stupas* also took numerous shapes. Featured in this exhibition are examples from China, Japan, and Tibet (figures 24-27). The steatite votive *stupa* is one of the earliest examples from China (figure 24). Dating to 435 of the Northern Liang Period (397-460), the reliquary is rendered in the Indic cylindrical form in three sections. The top and bottom sections are carved with Buddha and Bodhisattva images while the midsection bears a Buddhist text in Chinese. Perhaps the most interesting elements of this *stupas* are the Chinese trigrams, the three horizontal lines, continuous or broken, above the standing figures in the bottom section. These are concerned with the cosmic forces of *yin* and *yang* and their interactive dynamic. The presence of the trigrams suggests a commingling of indigenous Chinese and Buddhist traditions, which enhances the object's magical potency. The Northern Liang princes were devout Buddhists, and the discovery of several similar votive *stupas* from the Gansu and Turfan regions has been attributed to their patronage of Buddhism. Another Chinese example of the votive *stupa* dates to the Tang dynasty (618-907) (figure 27). Cast in bronze with gilt silver, the reliquary is in the Indic shape with a dome surmounted by a mast with five umbrellas and a bud-shaped finial. The dome is engraved with bands of fine lines. The round drum is supported on a waisted stem with a widely splayed foot. Two other reliquaries associated with Buddhist sovereigns are included in the exhibit. The small wooden *stupa* simply rendered with three discs and a parasol is one of a million miniature reliquaries, each inserted with a small printed *dharani* charm, commissioned by Empress Shōtoku of Japan in gratitude after the suppression of a rebellion in 764 (figure 26). The other reliquary, dated 955, is one of 84,000 commissioned by King Qian Hongshu of the Wuyue Kingdom of China. It consists of a square base surmounted by four acroteria (a central mast is missing in this example) and is cast in bronze with motifs of *jatakas* (stories of the Buddha's previous lives), Buddha figures, and guardian deities (figure 25).

IMAGES

In early Indian Buddhist narratives, the Buddha was not represented but was indicated by symbols such as his footprints, his throne, or the bodhi tree to mark his presence. Anthropomorphic images of the Buddha were created in the first century of the common era. Some of these early images functioned like the *stupa*, as a reminder of the physical presence of the Buddha, and thus of his deeds and his path of enlightenment as a model for worshipers. However, the cult of images certainly developed in conjunction with the deification of the Buddha and the development of Bud-

Figure 31 (top left)
Banner Painting of Standing Guanyin Attended by Two Donors
China
Tang Dynasty (618-907) to Five Dynasties Period (907-960)
c. 9th-10th century
Courtesy of the Arthur M. Sackler Museum
Harvard University Art Museums
First Fogg Expedition to China,1923-1924

Figure 32 (bottom left)
Bodhisattva Guanyin
China
Tang Dynasty (618-907)
7th-8th century
gilt bronze
Asian Art Museum of San Francisco
Gift of Mr. and Mrs. Alexander D. Calhoun, Jr.

Figure 33 (top right)
Eleven-headed Kannon
Japan
Late Heian (794-1185)-early Kamakura Period (1185-1333)
12th century
bronze
The Cleveland Museum of Art
Gift of Mrs. John Lyon Collyer in memory of her mother, Mrs. G. M. G. Forman

Figure 34 (bottom right)
Bodhisattva Avalokiteshvara
Nepal
13th century
gilt bronze, semi-precious stones
Harn Museum of Art Collection
Museum purchase, gift of Michael A. Singer

29

Figure 35
Shōtoku Taishi as a Child
Japan
Kamakura Period (1185-1333)
early 14th century
joined wood, black lacquer, traces of color, crystal
The Cleveland Museum of Art
Gift of Mr. and Mrs. James Campbell Weir
in memory of
Dr. and Mrs. William Hawksley Weir

dhism into a popular religion in the Mahayana. The representation of the Buddha is not a realistic portrayal of him as a mortal person but as a superhuman being who has extraordinary wisdom. The Buddha image is therefore an idealized depiction of the accomplishment of spiritual perfection through the human form.

The Buddha is said to have thirty-two distinguishing marks (*lakshanas*), including a cranial protuberance (*ushnisha*), long earlobes, three ring marks on his neck, and webbed feet. Since the Buddha advocated the ideal of monasticism, he is depicted wearing a monk's robe. The Buddha is shown either standing or seated; when seated, his feet are crossed in the yoga, or meditating, position. His hand gestures, called *mudras*, codify symbolic meanings and include the *abhaya mudra* (with the right hand raised, palm outward) that reassures or gives blessing; the *dhyana*, or meditation, *mudra* (with hands folded in the lap); and the *bhumisparsa*, or earth-touching, *mudra* (with the right hand reaching down, palm inward) that recalls the critical moment before enlightenment when the Buddha called upon the earth to witness his victory. Later in India, canonical proportions were devised to express the ideal anatomy of the Buddha.

Statues or pictorial images of the Buddha were enshrined in temples or cave shrines for worship throughout all of Buddhist Asia. Although the iconography of the Buddha remained constant, there was much diversity in style and regional characteristics. Small images that functioned as personal devotional icons also demonstrated variations from medium to style; examples in this exhibit are drawn from China, Korea, Thailand, and Indonesia (figures 28-30). Placed on home altars or hung on walls, these icons received prayers and offerings of flowers and incense. In Thailand, worshipers also made donations by placing gold coins inside the hollow image or applying gold leaf onto the statue.

The Bodhisattva ideal is a principal tenet of Mahayana Buddhism. In contrast to the Buddha, who wears a monk's robe, Bodhisattvas are shown as princely figures adorned with crowns and jewels, modeled after Gautama's role as a prince before he gained enlightenment. The great Bodhisattvas became some of the most popular savior figures of devotional Buddhism. Among them Avalokiteshvara (called Guanyin in Chinese, Kwannon in Korean, and Kannon in Japanese), the Bodhisattva of Compassion, was the most important (figures 31-34). Avalokiteshvara, literally "the lord who sees the world," can manifest in thirty-three forms, both male and female. The deity is worshiped and invoked in times of perils such as fire, drowning, or robbery. Women often prayed to the Bodhisattva to grant them children. In the banner painting from Dunhuang, China (figure 31), the standing Bodhisattva is shown with the pious donor and donatrice, who are making offerings. The Japanese example (figure 33) bears eleven heads, a Tantric form of Avalokiteshvara, while the exquisite four-armed Nepalese piece (figure 34) demonstrates yet another manifestation of the Bodhisattva. Corresponding to Avalokiteshvara's thirty-three forms, a circuit of thirty-three temples was established in Japan as the pilgrimage route for Kannon devotionalism. A block-printed pilgrim's map lists these thirty-three numinous places, shown with images of Kannon, or the Bodhisattva, in different forms (plate 8).

Other Buddhist icons in the exhibit include a small image of Prajnaparamita, a Tantric female deity personifying the perfection of wisdom (plate 9). It is beautifully crafted in copper with copper and silver inlay, as well as inset semiprecious stones.

Historical persons in the Buddhist tradition may also become deified and worshiped as personal deities. In Japan, a major cult evolved around Prince Shōtoku (574-622), the preeminent statesman who established the Buddhist faith as the religion of the land. A favorite portrayal of Prince Shōtoku as a cult image shows him at the age of two, when he proclaimed his devotion to Buddhism (figure 35). Dressed in a red skirt, the infant is depicted with hands clasped in prayer. In Tibet, devotees commissioned images of their teachers, which were worshiped to emphasize spiritual lineage from master to pupil. The gilt bronze figure inset with turquoise and silver (plate 10) has been identified as Yongs-'dzin ngag-dbang bzang-po (1546-1615), an abbot and famous scholar of the Kagyu sect.

VOTIVE TABLETS, TALISMANS, AND CHARMS

Votive tablets, or plaques, are usually small images of the Buddha or other deities stamped on clay from pottery or metal molds and then baked or sun-dried. Like terra cotta miniature *stupas*, votive tablets are inexpensively produced in large quantities at temples or other pilgrimage sites. Worshipers or pilgrims purchase these tablets to offer at the holy sites or keep them as personal icons or souvenirs.

The practice of making votive tablets, alongside that of votive *stupas*, originated in India around the beginning of the common era, but became popular during the Gupta (320-647) and Pala (c. 730-c. 1197) periods. There are two types of votive tablets: one portrays Buddhist figures; the other, called *dharani* sealings, bears a magical Buddhist formula or verse. The latter type, like the votive *stupas* stamped with a Buddhist creed, are usually found inside *stupas* or other sacred monuments for consecration purposes. Votive tablets are found in and around *stupa* and temple sites or in caves used for seclusion or meditation. One favorite motif on these tablets is the Buddha seated under the Mahabodhi Temple and the bodhi tree, his hands in the earth-touching gesture. Many examples dating to the tenth and eleventh centuries have been found. The Pala style of these votive tablets was closely followed in Thailand during the tenth century and in Burma during the Pagan Period from the twelfth to the fourteenth century.

Votive *stupas* and votive tablets were among the first mass-produced objects of devotion. In addition to the multiplication of *stupas* or images for the sake of accumulating religious merit, the reduplication of Buddhas corresponded to the Mahayana notion of numerous Buddhas. The motif of Thousand Buddhas, represented in relief carvings or in murals of cave-temples, expressed the notion that Buddhahood was eternal and omnipresent. In conjunction with the practices of meditation and reciting Buddhist phrases or the names of Buddhas, the sheer number of these images attained a mystical efficacy. Furthermore, stamping the image of the Buddha repeatedly was a pious, devotional deed likened to counting the rosary. Images of the Buddha were stamped on sand, clay, or paper. The exercise of printing images (see below), painting numerous icons, or writing out many Buddhist phrases every day were similar devotional activities. Two examples from the Edo Period (1615-1868) are the Zen monk Hakuin Ekaku's calligraphy (figure 36), and the painting of Kitano Tenjin, a deified cultural figure and patron-saint of scholarship worshiped in Buddhist-Shinto contexts (figure 37).

Amulets, also made of clay or other materials, are smaller versions of votive tablets. They are worn on the body for protective purposes. In Thailand and in Tibet the use of Buddhist amulets developed into major cults that have survived into modern times. Those from Thailand feature Buddhist deities, kings, and forest saints. Today they are widely sold and collected, and almost every Thai wears one. In Tibet, Buddhist amulets are commonly known as *tsha-tsha*. They feature a wide range of deities, both benign and ferocious, from the pantheon of esoteric Buddhism. Those made from clay mixed with ashes or pulverized bones of incarnate lamas are highly valued as talismans. These amulets are placed on home altars, carried in charm boxes called *ga'u*, or enshrined in rough shelters in open air. A particularly beautiful *ga'u* box, which contains an amulet of the Bodhisattva Manjusri, is cast in silver with floral decorations and Buddhist iconography (figure 11). Another exquisite example of an enshrined amulet comes from Edo Period Japan (figure 38). Shaped in the form of a lotus petal, the miniature shrine opens to reveal relief representations of the Historical Buddha Shakyamuni (Japanese: Shaka Nyorai) preaching the Buddhist Law while seated on a lotus throne. The Buddha is flanked by two attendant Bodhisattvas: Manjusri (Japanese: Monju Bosatsu), riding a lion, and Samantabhadra (Japanese: Fugen Bosatsu), riding an elephant, all amidst stylized clouds. The carving of the tiny interior figures is quite detailed, enhanced with polychromy and gilt against the natural grain of the fragrant sandalwood. The exterior of the shrine is decorated with motifs of lotus petals and the Sanskrit seed character for Shakyamuni in gold lacquer on a gunmetal-gray lacquer ground. Such shrines were made in many sizes, but this small one was probably intended to be carried as an amulet (perhaps by a warrior into battle).

The process of stamping images on clay and other materials was no doubt a precursor to printing on paper. With the advent of woodblock printing and the invention of paper, block printed images or charms became another important

Figure 36 (left)
Hakuin Ekaku
Japanese (1685-1769)
Calligraphy with the Posthumous Name of Prince Shōtoku
Edo Period (1615-1868), 18th century
ink on paper
Private collection, Cambridge, Massachusetts

Figure 37 (right)
Konoe Nobutada
Japanese (1565-1614)
Kitano Tenjin
Momoyama Period (1573-1615)
ink on paper
Private collection, Cambridge, Massachusetts

Figure 38 (top)
(exterior and interior views)
Miniature Shrine in the Form of a Lotus Petal
Japan, Edo Period (1615-1868)
late 18th-early 19th century
sandalwood, polychromy, gilt
Courtesy of the Arthur M. Sackler Museum
Harvard University Art Museums
Gift of Dorothy A. Heath and Milan A. Heath, Jr.
Class of 1959, in honor of John M. Rosenfield

Figure 39 (center)
Amulet Worn by Shugendo Practitioner
(detail)
Japan
Edo Period (1615-1868)
woodblock print on paper
Private collection, Cambridge, Massachusetts

Figure 40 (bottom)
Dharma Master rDo rje seng ge
Tibetan (1152-1220)
Book Cover with Buddhist Deities
Nepal or Tibet
c. 15th century
wood, polychromy, gilt
Courtesy of the Arthur M. Sackler Museum
Harvard University Art Museums

medium for fashioning devotional objects. The sealed library of the Dunhuang cave-temples in northwestern China has yielded many Buddhist prints dating from the ninth century, featuring devotional icons such as Avalokiteshvara. Long scrolls were made of joined sheets of paper impressed with images of Buddha and Bodhisattvas. One notation recorded that twenty-one images were printed on certain days of each month. From China the practice spread to Japan, where blocks were usually carved with multiple images of ten or one hundred. Devotees paid for the printing, but the temple retained the printed sheets and put them as bundles inside wooden images. Placing these printed images inside statues established a link between the donors and the divinities represented by the statues. Small sheets printed with Buddhist phrases, as magical emblems of the Buddha's teachings, were placed inside votive *stupas* of East Asia (see figures 25-26).

Small rolls of printed images also served as amulets. The amulet in figure 39 was probably worn by a practitioner of the Japanese Shugendo, a Buddhist creed that emphasizes austere practices such as mountaineering. The amulet contains a long roll of stamped images; the section illustrated shows the Sixteen Benign Deities who guard the *Heart Sutra*. A short version of the *Perfection of Wisdom Sutra*, the *Heart Sutra* was particularly known for its magical efficacy. The cult of the *Heart Sutra* was advocated by Xuanzang (600-664), the celebrated Chinese pilgrim and translator who traveled to India to bring back Buddhist scriptures. Xuanzang is shown here as an itinerant monk; his role in spreading the Buddhist faith afforded him a place among the supernatural deities.

BOOKS

The Buddha's teachings were first transmitted orally for several centuries. During the Maurya period (322-185 B.C.E.) in India, Buddhist texts began to be written down in Pali and then in other vernaculars. With the development of the Mahayana, Sanskrit became the canonical language for composing new scriptures. As Buddhism spread to the rest of Asia, the Buddhist canon was translated into many languages, from Chinese to Tibetan and Mongolian. Since the scriptures preserve the teachings of the Buddha, the book also became the object of devotional worship. Two texts were particularly worshiped as cult objects: the *Perfection of Wisdom Sutra* in South Asia and the Himalayas, and the *Lotus Sutra* in East Asia. Both were considered the final scriptural statement of Mahayana philosophy. The *Lotus Sutra* was worshiped like a relic in Japan, where scrolls of the text were placed in cylindrical reliquaries and then buried in sutra mounds. In the eleventh and twelfth centuries of Pala India, the art of the book reached a peak when lavish copies of Buddhist texts written on palm leaves and embellished with illuminated manuscripts were commissioned. The illuminations depict transcendental Buddhas, Bodhisattvas, and other divinities; not necessarily related to the texts, these divine figures served as foci of meditation and devotion in Tantric practices. Devotees commissioned these Buddhist texts as a pious deed, bringing merit to all associated with the production, from the donors to the painters and the monasteries where the *sutras* were enshrined. The art of the book was destroyed in India with the Muslim invasion in the twelfth century, but the tradition continued in Nepal and Tibet, where the text became increasingly worshiped as a mystical cult object. Book covers were often fashioned in wood and carved with Buddhist divinities (figure 40).

Although Buddhism declined in India after the Muslim conquest, the religion continued to be a vital spiritual force in many Asian countries, especially in Japan, Thailand, Sri Lanka, Burma, and Tibet. In China, Buddhism suffered a major setback in the persecution of 845, but survived in the form of Chan (known as Zen in Japanese) Buddhism and in folk Buddhist practices that later commingled with local cults. Buddhism was introduced to the West at the end of the nineteenth century. Combining modern scholarship on Buddhism, Buddhists in countries East and West continue traditional forms of devotional worship as well as religious practices such as meditation.

Dorothy C. Wong
Assistant Professor
McIntire Department of Art
University of Virginia

Figure 41 (above)
Seated Female Figure (Esi Mansa)
Ghana, Akan People (Fante)
wood, paint, patina
Harn Museum of Art Collection
Gift of Rod McGalliard

Figure 42 (opposite)
Shango Staff (oshe Shango)
Nigeria, Yoruba People
wood, patina
Harn Museum of Art Collection
Gift of the Center for African Studies, University of Florida

THE ARTS OF PERSONAL DEVOTION

in African Religion

THE MANY NUANCES TO THE UNDERSTANDING OF THE SACRED IN THE INNUMERABLE VARIATIONS OF AFRICAN RELIGIONS MAKE IT DIFFICULT TO GENERALIZE, BUT AS A RULE THE SUPERNATURAL IS NOT FIXED IN AFRICAN THOUGHT. NOT ONLY ARE THERE HUNDREDS OF VARIATIONS OF INDIGENOUS SYSTEMS FOR ADDRESSING THE SUPERNATURAL OR THE SACRED, BUT VARIOUS INTERPRETATIONS OF ISLAM AND CHRISTIANITY HAVE BEEN AT WORK ON THE CONTINENT FOR CENTURIES.

In most indigenous religions no real boundaries exist between the world of the visible and the invisible, the sacred and the not sacred. The two realms coexist and interact. Although there is usually a priesthood, ordinary people have access to spiritual beings, and spirits act in the lives of individual humans.

Although most African religions hold that a supreme Creator God established the universe and is lord of both spiritual and human realms, individuals seldom interact with this aloof being. This is not to say that the Creator God is not accessible or is not interested in the created, but devotion is normally directed to any of a number of lesser gods or spirits. These act on behalf of the Creator to support the community, the family, and the individual in coping with the intricacies of negotiating their ways in this world.

The exuberant singing, chanting, dancing, and ecstatic possession in which the worshiper interacts with the spirit contrasts with the sedate piety of devotional activities in most expressions of Western religion. Personal involvement of the devotee with the spirit may, in fact, involve the spirit "mounting" or possessing the worshiper, who temporarily becomes an ecstatic vehicle for the actions of the god in this world. The direct interaction of the spirit and the worshiper is a key aspect of much African religious practice. The devotion of the individual to the spirit is recognized not only through such energetic acts of praise but also through the proffering of gifts to the spirit. Shrines and altars are designated as meeting places between humans and the divine, special places where sacrifices and libations may be made to feed the spirit or where material objects may be presented as tokens of devotion. Both natural and created objects accumulate in shrines and on altars, stimulating the residents of the spiritual world into action or reminding them of the dedication of human followers. All sorts of objects, natural and created, may be placed in the shrine ensemble. Among the Akan peoples of Ghana, small figures may be offered to the deity as gifts or may serve as attributes of the spirit. Almost all Akan shrines are concerned either directly or indirectly with human fertility, and the numerous mother and child figures offered to the spirits underscore ideas of fertility, nourishment, family, and continuity (figure 41). The chalk-whitened surface of figures such as the Harn example has to do with the practice of powdering the body for religious activities to show respect and dedication to the deity.

GODS

Not all African religions have organized systems of gods, although some, like the Yoruba peoples of Nigeria, do have an extensive pantheon of gods called *orisha*. Although the *orisha* are said to be numberless, the individual worshiper has a specific god on whom he or she focuses attention and who is called upon for assistance in this world. One of the best known of these is Shango, the god of thunder. Like the lightning he is associated with, Shango can act capriciously and aggressively, yet he is exceedingly charitable to his followers, defending them and providing abundance and well-being.

A variety of forms may be used on the altar of Shango, depending on the desires of the worshipers who give them or the aims of the artist commissioned to create them. The most common form is a staff, the *oshe Shango* (figure 42), held and vigorously manipulated during dances in honor of the god. Priests who wield the instrument during celebratory festivals in Shango's honor emphasize their forceful gestures as they dance possessed by the deity or while they chant poetry in his praise.

The symbol that defines a Shango object is the double ax, a reference to Neolithic stone axes which are interpreted by the Yoruba to be thunderbolts hurled to earth by the vengeful god. The symbolic double ax form represents two thunder celts placed back to back, implying that Shango is able to strike in opposite directions simultaneously. The double ax, along with the two heads on many staffs, also alludes to the Yoruba belief in the power of doubling, a capacity often associated with Shango.

The Shango staff acts as a talisman for the devotee, attracting the god's protection and generosity. It is often placed among other ritual implements on the altar for Shango where routine sacrifices to the *orisha* are made. A cord passed through the hole in the handle allows the staff to be attached to the devotee's wrist as a protective device, hung over the doorway to invite the god's defense of the home, or suspended at the entrances of farms, asking Shango's blessing of abundant crops. While larger *oshe Shango* may be propped as freestanding altar sculptures, smaller personal ones such as this example may be gathered together in a calabash on Shango's altar.

SPIRITS

The differentiation between African divinities and spirits is not at all clear. Perhaps a spirit that is widely recognized and has many devotees will be called a god, especially if an organized priesthood looks after the affairs of the divinity. In addition, there seems to be an unending variety of spirit beings in African religions that are not always referred to as gods, including nature spirits, spirits of the dead, ancestor spirits, and spirits associated with qualities of the individual person.

Devotees try to communicate with spirits and to request their aid in getting on in the world. Individual spirits are considered to have human characteristics and may be addressed at shrines to ask for favors, for success, for well-being, and especially for children. Among the Akan peoples of Ghana, spirits are often beseeched for assistance in conception. A specific type of sculpture called an *akua'ba* has been created as an aid to fertility and as a plea for

Plate 1
The Virgin and Child with Donor
Book of Hours, Hours of the Virgin
France, Rouen
late 15th century
vellum, ink, tempera, cloth
The Pierpont Morgan Library, New York
ms. m. 167, f. 153

Plate 2
José Negrón
Puerto Rican, Corozal, b. 1928
Our Lady of Montserrat
Miracle of Hormigueros
1997
wood, polychromy
Lent from a private collection

Plate 3
Passover Goblet
Bohemia
1845-1865
glass
The Jewish Museum, New York
Gift of Dr. Harry G. Friedman

Gabriel Syren
German
Passover Plate
after 1727
pewter
The Jewish Museum, New York
Gift of Dr. Harry G. Friedman

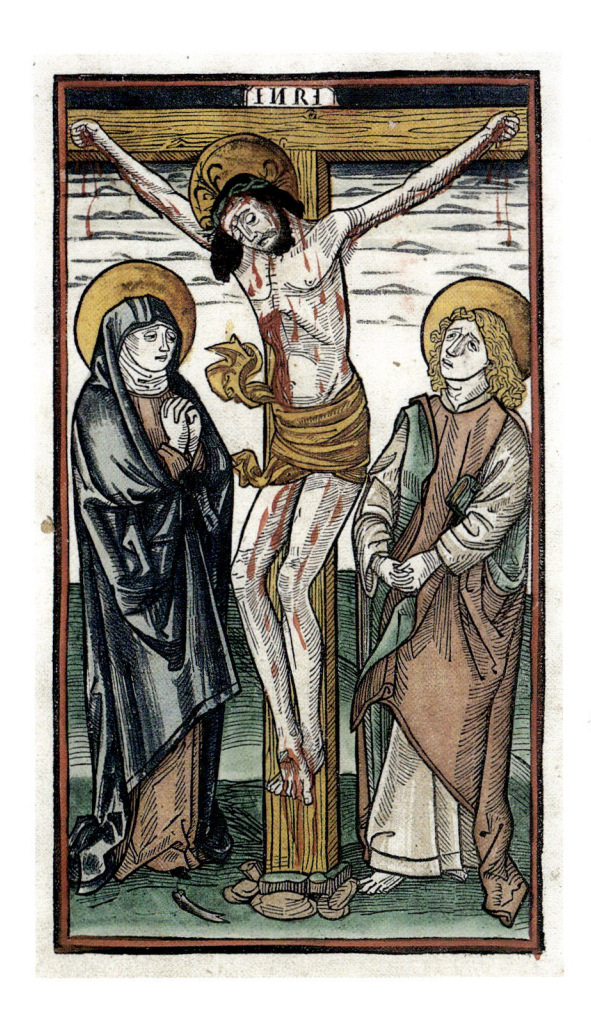

Plate 4 (left)
Christ on the Cross
Germany
1485
hand-colored woodcut
National Gallery of Art, Washington, D.C.
Rosenwald Collection

Plate 5 (right)
Crucifixion Panel **(from diptych)**
Northern France
14th century
ivory
Vanderbilt University Fine Arts Gallery
Gift of Mrs. Thomas Matthews

Plate 6 (top)
Koranic Amulet
Somalia, Xamar Weyn
18th century
silver, amber, red beads
Foundation for Cross-Cultural
Understanding, Washington, D.C.

Plate 7 (bottom)
Statuette of a Horse
Greece
8th century B.C.E.
bronze
The Cleveland Museum of Art
John L. Severance Fund

Plate 8 (left)
Print for Pilgrims
Japan
Edo Period (1615-1868)
woodblock print on paper
Lent by Drs. Geoffrey and Ming-mei Redmond

Plate 9 (right)
Prajnaparamita
Central Tibet
13th-14th century
copper alloy, copper and silver inlay, semi-precious stones, traces of paint
Virginia Museum of Fine Arts, Richmond
The Berthe and John Ford Collection, Gift of Berthe and John Ford

Plate 10
Lama, Yongs-'dzin-ngag-dbang bzang-po
Tibet
18th century
gilt bronze, turquoise, silver
Asian Art Museum of San Francisco
Gift of Raymond G. and Milla L. Handley

Plate 11
Spirit Spouse (blolo bla)
Ivory Coast, Baule People
wood, enamel
Harn Museum of Art Collection
Gift of Rod McGalliard

Plate 12
Reliquary Figure (mbulu)
Southeastern Gabon, Kota People
wood, brass, copper
Harn Museum of Art Collection
Museum purchase, funds provided by
Michael A. Singer

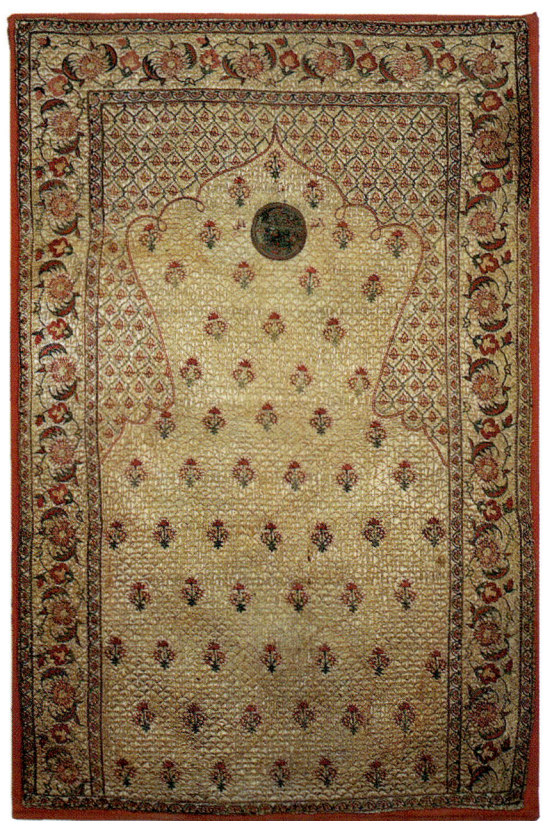

Plate 13 (left)
Prayer Rug
West Anatolia
c. 1850
wool
Lent by Mr. and Mrs. Jon M. Anderson

Plate 14 (right)
Mughal-style Prayer Rug
Northern India
c. 1800
silk and cotton fabric, embroidered with silk thread
Lent from a private collection

Figure 43 (left)
Fertility Figure (akua'ba)
Ghana, Akan People (Asante)
wood, wire, beads
Harn Museum of Art Collection
Gift of Rod McGalliard

Figure 44 (center)
Male Twin Statuettes (ere ibeji)
Nigeria, Yoruba People
wood, beads, leather, camwood patina
Harn Museum of Art Collection
Gift of Rod McGalliard

Figure 45 (right)
Personal Shrine for a Man (ikenga)
Nigeria, Ahoada area, Igbo People
wood, fiber, patina
Harn Museum of Art Collection
Gift of the Center for African Studies, University of Florida

Figure 46 (top)
Sande Society Helmet Mask (zogbe)
Sierra Leone, Gola People
wood, metal
Harn Museum of Art Collection
Gift of Rod McGalliard

Figure 47
Commemorative Vessel (abusua kuruwa)
Ghana, Akan People
terra cotta
Harn Museum of Art Collection
Gift of Rod McGalliard

conception (figure 43). A priest calls upon the spirit to encourage pregnancy and consecrates an *akua'ba* figure to ensure its efficacy. The figure becomes an object of personal devotion for the woman who carries it on her person as a vehicle of the power of the spirit. The *akua'ba* not only is believed to induce pregnancy but also to assure easy carriage and a safe delivery. Equally important are the ideals of Akan beauty the figure embodies. The smooth, broad, high forehead, the rounded, slightly flattened face, and the long, ringed neck embody Akan concepts of ideal beauty that are believed to be imparted to the child forming in the womb.

Not only do spirits interact with individuals in numerous ways, as in the granting of fertility, but there are also spirits that are themselves extensions of the being of the individual, considered to be aspects of that individual. The Baule people of Ivory Coast believe that everyone has a spirit lover, called *blolo bla* (spirit woman) or *blolo bian* (spirit man) in the spirit world *(blolo)* (plate 11). The individual is associated with the spirit lover in *blolo* before birth in this world, but after the person has been born on earth, recollection of the spirit mate is lost. In jealousy, the spirit may make its presence known by causing some type of personal misfortune. If it is determined through divination that the problem has been caused by the spirit lover, the diviner prescribes the carving of a sculptural representation of the offended spirit. Ideally beautiful, the figure serves as a temporary dwelling place for the spirit lover. Its long, ringed neck is a symbol of pride, honor, and elegance. Its clear eyes draw attention to a delicate face, reflecting the cultural ideals of beauty with its high forehead and well-styled hairdo. Indeed, the styled coiffure and the clothing, jewelry, and red nail polish indicate that this *blolo bla* is of good social standing. Two children added as attributes of the *blolo bla* here have to do with the Baule concept of children as wealth.

The earthly half of this spiritual couple cares for the figure in a shrine set up in the corner of his sleeping room, where he propitiates the spirit lover with gifts of food, money, perfume, or any other item the spirit entity is believed to appreciate. One night a week is reserved for the spirit during which the earthly spouse of the individual sleeps elsewhere to allow the spirit lover access to his or her earthly lover through dreams.

The concept of a spirit being as an extension of the self as exemplified by the Baule spirit lover figures has a somewhat different connotation among the Yoruba of Nigeria. Here each individual is believed to have not a spirit lover but a spirit double that played with him or her when they were in the spirit world *(orun)*. When the individual was born on earth, he or she lost cognizance of the spirit double. In the case of twins, both are said to be born on earth and to share a soul. The Yoruba have the world's highest rate of twin births. Twins are believed to have power comparable to that of the *orisha* (deities) and are thought to bring prosperity to the family if revered or misfortune if neglected. The mother of twins attains a position of high status, and she must live a ritual life dedicated to their care.

Early delivery and low birth weight cause a high infant mortality rate among twins. When a twin dies, a *babalawo* (diviner) recommends that the parents either erect a shrine for the twin *(oju ibeji)* or commission the carving of a twin statuette *(ere ibeji)* (figure 44). The shrine or statuette is intended to prevent the deceased twin from luring the live twin to *orun*, the spirit world. The figure, which is believed to house the soul of the deceased twin, is fed and bathed as if it were a living child. As part of her commitment to ritual solicitude, the mother dances in the marketplace with her live twins or with the carved figure and begs for alms. When the *ere ibeji* is not being ritually handled by the mother, it is placed on an altar in the mother's sleeping quarters or is carefully wrapped in cloth and placed in a calabash.

When the mother dies, care for the *ere ibeji* may be passed on to the living twin. Alternatively, the carving may be given to an *iya ibeji* (a mother of many twins who takes care of the *ere ibeji* of others). Among the Oyo Yoruba, twin figures may be placed on a Shango shrine, for not only is Shango the deity of thunder, as the god of doubling he is also the protector of twins.

Some spirit forces are associated with various parts of the person's body. A number of groups in southern Nigeria focus on the right arm or hand as a location of personal spiritual power. Among the Igbo, an object known as the *ikenga* serves as a man's personal shrine (figure 45). It incorporates ideas of the individual's ancestors and his destiny, but more importantly it refers to his right arm or hand, the locus of his strength, his will to achieve. A man's right arm

Figure 48
Power Figure (nkisi, phuungu)
Democratic Republic of Congo, Yaka People
wood, cloth, feathers
Harn Museum of Art Collection
Gift of Dr. and Mrs. Saul A. Geronemus

Figure 49
Power Figure (nkisi, phuungu)
Democratic Republic of Congo, Yaka People
wood, cloth
Harn Museum of Art Collection
Gift of Rod McGalliard

signifies ability and power, and all important tasks are done with his right arm. By the time he is married, a man will have attained a small personal *ikenga*, such as the one illustrated here, referred to as the altar to his right hand. After he consecrates it before members of his lineage or his age grade, the *ikenga* is imbued with the power to attract success. It is treated as a spirit being and is propitiated with personal prayers and offerings.

Another spirit whose direct and special association with the individual is represented in the *sowei* and *zogbe* masks used in the Sande society among a number of peoples in Sierra Leone (figure 46). Sande is a women's organization in charge of initiating young women into the ranks of womanhood and is also responsible for maintaining special sacred medicines (*halei*) for the community. At the heart of the community, Sande exerts social, religious, and political power. When a woman reaches a specific rank within the organization, she commissions a mask to represent her patron spirit. After the mask has been carved, she anoints it with *halei*, and she is the only person who can invoke its spirit. Such masks are used in the initiation of girls as well as in communicating ideas of Sande to the community at large. When a woman appears wearing the masquerade, she is both honoring and giving visible form to the spirit with whom she is closely associated.

SPIRITS OF THE DEAD

Although individual devotion to gods and spirits is common, meaningful connection with the supernatural may be demonstrated perhaps more easily in relation to communication with and honoring the spirits of the deceased. Among the Akan peoples of Ghana, special rites are performed by the family one week after a person's death. Food for the journey to the land of the ancestors is prepared in terra cotta pots crafted specifically for the occasion. Special commemorative vessels called *abusua kuruwa* play a significant role in funerary celebration (figure 47). The elaborate pot here has a figure atop the lid to represent the deceased. Specific characteristics refer to the role the individual played in life. The gun and cap on this example may indicate the deceased was a hunter or soldier. His ringed neck is symbolic of success and prosperity. The flattened egg-shaped head, a common feature in Akan sculpture, signifies ideal beauty.

During funeral rites, relatives of the deceased shave their heads and place the hair inside the commemorative receptacle, symbolizing clan unity to encourage the spirit of the departed to watch over them and help to maintain the family from its new perspective in the spirit world. Offerings of food, the hearthstones on which the food was prepared, and the *abusua kuruwa* are carried to a special place called the *asensie*, or "place of pots," located outside the city near the cemetery. The spirit of the deceased is believed to remain in this transitional zone for forty days before its departure to the world of spirits. On the first anniversary of the death, ritualistic washing consecrates the *abusua kuruwa* along with the other pots. The *abusua kuruwa* symbolizes the continuity of life in the ancestral realm and the role the spirit plays in the living family and serves as a libation vessel when descendants call upon the revered spirits of the dead.

Among the Kota peoples of southeastern Gabon it is not a specific ancestor who is called upon for aid but the collective force of the family dead. The relics of deceased family dignitaries are placed in a woven basket or bark box. These reliquaries, which contain the skulls and bones of deceased parents, lineage chiefs, or important healers, are topped by a stylized figure called *mbulu* (plate 12). This *mbulu* figure is made of wood and plated with brass strips arranged on a diagonal. Metal forms the eyes and nose, and the abstract mouth is engraved into a brass strip that bisects the leaf-shaped concave face. The "shine" of the copper and brass, which is achieved by scrubbing the metal with sand, is believed to augment the power of the *mbulu* figure to repel negative forces. Members of the lineage consult the reliquary when problems arise or before important events.

In many parts of central Africa, the powers of the dead may work in other objects known as *minkisi* (singular, *nkisi*). These power objects contain many ingredients, sometimes the earth from the grave of a powerful person. They have the capacity to heal or to harm—a power that emanates from the medicinal accouterments attached to the figure. The two *nkisi* figures shown here are from the Yaka people of the Democratic Republic of Congo (figures 48, 49). Referred

Figure 50
Ancestral Head (uhumwelao)
Nigeria, Benin, Edo People
terra cotta
Harn Museum of Art Collection
Gift of Rod McGalliard

to as *phuungu*, this specific type on *nkisi* is believed to have the power to protect the individual from witches and enemies. The medicinal materials for protection are packed into a ball-like form that envelops the torso of one figure, and in an attachment of feathers and cloth tightly wrapped with string around the other. Blood sacrifice performed at the creation of the *phuungu* and subsequent offerings result in the accumulation of patina on the figures. Kept by the head of a patrilineage and passed from father to son, *phuungu* serve as personalized focal points in rituals that control and neutralize malevolent influences and encourage benevolent forces.

ANCESTOR SPIRITS

In most African religions ancestors are special cases of the spirits of the dead. Ancestors are individuals who played a significant role in the family and the community while they were living on earth. They must have living descendants who have observed the appropriate rites to install them in the appropriate level in the spirit world and who continue to communicate with them through ritual. Ancestors remain close to the living, bestowing fertility, health, prosperity, and security upon their family and punishing them if neglected.

The head is a pertinent spiritual symbol of the individual's own spirit among some Nigerian peoples such as the Edo and the Yoruba. The head symbolizes life and behavior in this world, the potential to organize one's actions in such a way as to endure and flourish. An individual's head is the site of thinking and judgment. It is the locus of will, character, hearing, seeing, and speaking. An individual's fortunes may depend on the successful coordination of these faculties. Representations of heads are used in several contexts in the kingdom of Benin in southern Nigeria. In the Edo kingdom, heads of clay, wood, or brass were placed on the graves of ancestors of families of specific categories (figure 50). Wooden heads were used on the ancestral altars of chiefs, clay heads on those of the brass casters' guild, and brass heads on the royal ancestral altars in the palace. Scholars seem to disagree on the function of the heads, called *uhumwelao*. Some suggest they are merely decorative. Others purport that they do not have spiritual power but are purely commemorative. Still others state that they once functioned directly in ancestor rituals, serving as the temporary dwelling place of the ancestral spirit during the ritual of sacrifices and receiving the blood of the sacrificial animal. Regardless of its actual function, the head is perceived as the controller of one's destiny and plays an important role on Edo altars. The ancestor was lovingly called upon to aid the family and the individual at fixed times in the ritual calendar or in times of crisis.

Robin Poynor
Professor of Art History
University of Florida

Figure 51 (left to right)
Koshari Katsina Doll (Hano Clown)
Native American
First Mesa, Hopi, Southwest Region
c. 1880-1890
cottonwood root, pigments
Florida Museum of Natural History

Kachin-mana Katsina Doll (Kachina Maiden)
Native American
First Mesa, Hopi, Southwest Region
c. 1880-1890
cottonwood root, pigments
Florida Museum of Natural History

Heheya Katsina Doll (Farmer)
Native American
First Mesa, Hopi, Southwest Region
c. 1880-1890
cottonwood root, pigments
Florida Museum of Natural History

Koyemsi Katsina Doll (Mud Head)
Native American
First Mesa, Hopi, Southwest Region
c. 1880-1890
cottonwood root, pigments
Florida Museum of Natural History

MOST HESITATION

Is Not Without History

PART 1: HESITATION

I WAS VERY HESITANT ABOUT PARTICIPATING IN THE EXHIBITION **INTIMATE RITUALS AND PERSONAL DEVOTIONS** AND WAS MENTALLY CONSTRUCTING A GRACEFUL DECLINE AS LARRY PERKINS AND I WALKED DOWN THE HALLWAY OF THE HARN MUSEUM TO VIEW THE OBJECTS. AS WE LOOKED AT THEM, MY THOUGHTS WERE THAT THEY WERE NOT OUT OF THE ORDINARY FOR A "SACRED COLLECTION"—GHOST DANCE SHIRT, KATSINAS (FIGURE 51), AND AMULETS. • THE OBJECTS WERE SET OUT ON A TABLE, CATALOGUED, SOME WITH THE NUMBERS WRITTEN ON THEM. WHEN I LOOK AT COLLECTIONS I ALWAYS WONDER ABOUT ACQUISITION. WERE THE UMBILICAL AMULETS SOLD BECAUSE THE FAMILY NEEDED MONEY? WERE THE "SACRED" KATSINAS AND GHOST DANCE SHIRT ACTUALLY PART OF MASS PRODUCTION TO FULFILL THE NEEDS OF THE COLLECTORS OF THE SACRED? HAD THEY BEEN SOLD TO THE COLLECTOR BY INDIVIDUALS WHO HAD LOST FAITH, OR HAD THEY BEEN STOLEN? • **MOST HESITATION IS NOT WITHOUT HISTORY.**

PART 2: UNINVITED GUESTS AND LIVING ARTIFACTS

The absence of Christianity was an indicator that assimilation of aboriginal people was necessary for the creation of, "One nation under God." The people who had fled religious persecution were now denying aboriginal people their religious freedom. Aboriginal people were directed to give up the old ways and become "civilized." Laws were passed, and food rations withheld if tribal people did not comply.

It is interesting that this forced assimilation also simultaneously created a furious fever of collecting authentic aboriginal artifacts. The disappearing Indian was not vanishing because of natural reasons, rather the words "vanishing" and "disappearing" were colonial words for acts that were paving the way for the discipline of anthropology.

The latter part of the 1800s witnessed the development of anthropology in which careers were based on the zealous gathering and collecting of aboriginal objects and information, all aimed at the creation of a new authority, that of the "Tribal Expert" and the "Ethnologist." Many government subsidized expeditions which set out to document and census the "vanishing Indian" with photographers and painters were intent on capturing images of the last "primitives." Individual collectors bought every "authentic" knickknack that happened to be in an aboriginal home.

During this frantic gathering, graves were looted and ceremonial objects stolen or sold without group consensus. To meet the demand, artifacts were often created for sale. The market demands created spurious artifacts with appropri-

Figure 52
Umbilical Amulet in Shape of a Lizard **(top)**
Native American
Crow, Great Plains Region
c. 1910
buckskin, seed beads, cotton thread, sweetgrass, tin, horsehair, muslin
Florida Museum of Natural History

Umbilical Amulet in Shape of a Horny Toad **(bottom)**
Native American
Lakota, Great Plains Region
c. 1880
buckskin, seed beads, cotton thread, sweetgrass, tin
Florida Museum of Natural History

ate histories to satisfy the collector's need to own a part of the disappearing. Now, as a result, both sacred objects and the "manufactured sacred" are displayed side by side in museum collections.

I remember as a child in Oklahoma, family members recalling how they misled an anthropologist about sacred rites and rituals as a method of protecting the true sacred. Give the researchers a good story, and they would leave one in peace, then again....

On August 1, 1879, Frank Cushing accompanied the Stevenson expedition to Zuni, where he stayed for five years.

> By the end of December, the Stevenson expedition had returned to Washington. Only Cushing remained. Cushing entered another world, that of the Zuni.... The Governor of the Zuni, Palowahtiwa (Patricio Pino), was not at all pleased that Cushing remained. He directed Cushing to take off his white man's clothes, put on the mixed costume of a Spanish-Navaho, and try to blend in as much as possible. Cushing did that and more. He gradually came to understand the deep complexity of Zuni life. He was one of the first American ethnologists to immerse himself in another culture. He learned the language and their customs, and to most people, including the Zuni and maybe even himself, he became Zuni.[1]

So Native had Cushing become that he claimed to be always dressed in traditional Zuni attire. This amused the community, for in their information gathering they noticed that whenever Cushing put on his native attire, his friends from out of town would soon arrive to visit him—otherwise he was dressed like everyone else, that is to say in contemporary clothing.

Cushing relentlessly gathered information to the point of being rude. There are stories that he demanded to be part of ceremonies. Frank was a nuisance to the community with his constant poking and prodding. His presence was tolerated in order not to cause trouble with the authorities. As for the acceptance of Frank as a Zuni, by all Zuni, I am rather skeptical.

It is one thing to have a visitor who stays a bit longer than expected but to be dubbed a living artifact is another perspective that needs to be reevaluated. Take for instance Ishi, "the last of the Yahi," who was "found" on August 29, 1911: "a pathetic figure crouched upon the floor.... His feet were almost as wide as they were long, showing plainly that he had never worn either moccasins or shoes."[2] And "He was the last of his tribe...feared people...wandered, alone, like a hunted animal.... The man is as aboriginal in his mode of life as though he inhabited the heart of an African jungle, all of his methods are those of primitive peoples."[3]

Ishi was a dream come true for anthropologists and journalists. Just as America had been discovered, so had Ishi. Ignored was the possibility of Native-to-Native contact as in a story illustrated by Maidu artist Frank Day.[4]

As a child Frank often accompanied his father, and on one walk they came upon two Native men, one wounded and the other doctoring the wound. Both parties nodded acknowledgment, and each continued on their paths. Later, Frank's father was asked to communicate with Ishi, who had just been found in Oroville. Frank accompanied his father and recognized Ishi as the one who had been doctoring the wounded man. He later illustrated the Native-to-Native encounter before Oroville in his career as a painter.

Ishi spent the last years of his life as a resident of the Phoebe Apperson Hearst Museum of Anthropology under the anthropological study of museum director Alfred Kroeber (1909-1947).[5]

> Kroeber pointed out that 'he (Ishi) has perceptive powers far keener than those of highly educated white men. He reasons well, grasps an idea quickly, has a keen sense of humor, is gentle, thoughtful, and courteous and has a higher type of mentality than most Indians.' Thomas Waterman administered psychological tests and concluded in a newspaper interview that 'this wild man has a better head on him than a good many college men.'[6]

> His (Ishi's) survivance, that sense of mediation in tribal stories, is heard in a word that means 'one of the people', and that word became his name. So much the better, and he never told the anthropologists, reporters, and curious practitioners his sacred tribal name, not even his nicknames.[7]

Aside from all the official documenting of Ishi, I prefer the painting of Frank Day. Despite all the foraging of the sacred and mundane, to label, catalogue, and possess a living person as an artifact, the anthropologists still did not have a clue to the core of aboriginal continuance. Though sacred items were sold, stolen, and traded, what was always overlooked was the power that remained—and remains today as the core of Native continuance—that of Faith.

America was not the only country obsessed with control issues. In 1884 the Canadian government outlawed the potlatch feasts held on the Northwest Coast. (Over a period of days, oral histories were validated and shared at these large gatherings through dancing, singing, story telling, and abundant gift giving.) As a consequence, in 1921, at a famous potlatch held by Daniel Cramner, 45 people were arrested and were later released, but only after surrendering all their potlatch articles. All Native nations were affected one way or another by outside law.

As I said before, my hesitation was not without history.

PART 3: CONTEMPLATION

Yet Larry spoke with such sincerity that I finally agreed to be part of the project on the condition that repatriation of the exhibition's objects be considered if necessary. (The Florida Museum of Natural History has complied with the requirements of the Native American Graves and Repatriation Act. Larry David Perkins)

My expertise is in the field of photography, fine art imagery, and documentary, with emphasis on the Native community as my audience. Although in my travels I have viewed many collections, I do not claim to have extensive knowledge in the field of collections or feel that just because I am indigenous that I can interpret all indigenous sacred items, e.g., katsina. What I do possess, however, is an aboriginal view of collections, contemporary and historical family and personal information that would not fit on a 3 x 5 index card, information that is beyond date of purchase, amount paid, place of purchase. Fortunately, I was able to meet with individuals who possess expert knowledge of objects to be exhibited. Not only did we view the photographs of the objects but, we discussed the need to own the sacred.

In September I traveled to Sioux Falls, North Dakota, to meet with five other colleagues who were being honored with the Community Spirit Awards for integrating art and community. It was a perfect time to gather information.

Over breakfast I met with a brilliant young Cheyenne woman, Nicco Strange Owl, whose background is collections, and I immediately felt her passion for her work. She scrutinized the photographs I handed her, and while she was looking at them I told her my mixed feelings about participating in the exhibition and my concerns about the pieces. I expressed my worry about the pipe bowls and stems and wondered about their possible repatriation. After finishing her survey of the photographs she looked up at me and smiled.

Figure 53
***Ghost Dance Shirt* (back side)**
Native American
Lakota, Great Plains Region
c. 1890
cloth, polychromy, eagle feathers
Florida Museum of Natural History

First we started with questions around the umbilical pouches (figure 52). Nicco commented, "I don't know why someone would want to own a stranger's belly button." She went on, "The horny toad amulet signifies that the umbilical cord of a baby girl is inside and the lizard is for a baby boy. The amulets would be made for the child and hung from its cradle board, later used as a necklace." Evidence of the mother and child connection, the amulets are still made, celebrating the relationship.

"You know about the Ghost Dance?" I replied that I did, that it is was religion born out of survival. That the prophet Wovoka had had a dream at a time when dreams were especially needed.

In 1889, Wovoka, otherwise known as Jack Wilson (1856-1932), from the Nevada Paiute tribe, dreamt that Native people killed by the directive of Manifest Destiny would rise and that the foreigners, the white people, would be defeated and the land would once again be Native-controlled. The Ghost Dance gave hope to many tribes. It was believed if one embraced the vision of Wovoka, if one danced, had visions, and had faith, then the shirts and dresses they wore would be bullet-proof. Word spread quickly about the Ghost Dance, from Nevada to the plains, believers danced for their lives and the lives of their families.

> All Indians must dance, everywhere, keep on dancing. Pretty soon in next spring Great Spirit come. He bring back all game of every kind. The game be thick everywhere. All dead Indians come back and live again. They all be strong just like young men, be young again. Old blind Indians see again and get young again and have fine time. When Great Spirit comes this way, then all the Indians go to mountains, high up away from whites. Whites can't hurt Indians then. Then while Indians way up high, big flood comes like water and all white people die, get drowned. After that, water go away and then nobody but Indians everywhere and game all kinds thick. Then medicine man tell Indians to send word to all Indians to keep up dancing and the good time will come. Indians who don't dance, who don't believe in this word, will grow little, just about a foot high and stay that way. Some of them will be turned into wood and be burned in fire. Wovoka, Paiute Messiah[8]

"You must not hurt anybody or do harm to anyone. You must not fight. Do right always."[9]

The dancing and depth of faith of the participants made the authorities so nervous that they ordered the dancing to stop. What I find very interesting here is the threatening power of faith and how it made, and still makes, people nervous. The deep faith in the Ghost Dance was unfathomable. But alas the shirts did not work at the 1890 Wounded Knee Massacre, and more than 200 people died.

The Ghost Dance was short-lived for obvious reasons, but shirts and dresses riddled with bullet holes and covered with blood were collected by anthropologists, curio collectors, and the amused. Native families disposed of Ghost Dance clothing in disgust; they had been deceived, and who would want to keep evidence of being deceived?

I asked Nicco about the complications of exhibiting the shirt (figure 53). She said that after much talk, the general consensus of her group was that the power of the shirt was in the past, that now it is just a piece of clothing. She also added that a majority of the Ghost Dance shirts in collections were fake. The demand for authentic objects by collectors had created imitations.

It is a reality that collections do possess manufactured sacred items. The value and demand for collectible objects was recognized by the community, and many people started to create art. This was another way of protecting the sacred while also empowering the community.

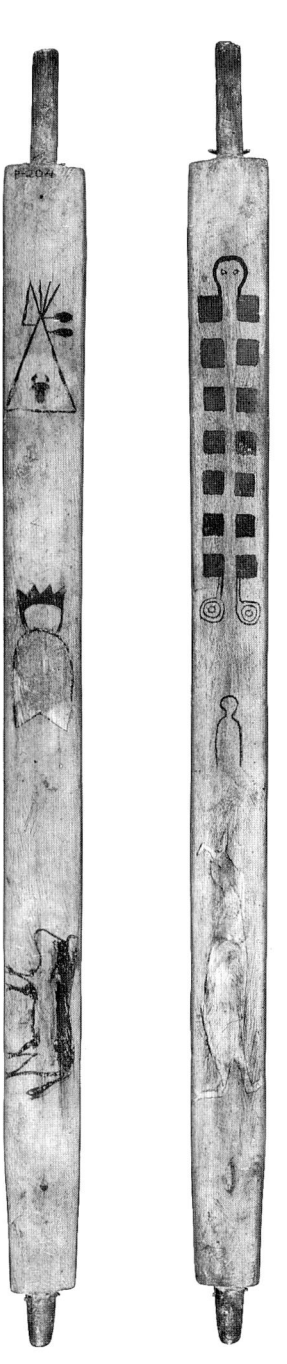

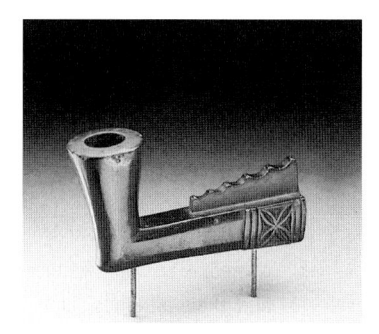

Figure 54 (left)
Pipe Stem (side 1)
Native American
Lakota, Great Plains Region
c. 1880
wood, pigment
Florida Museum of Natural History

Figure 55 (center)
Pipe Stem (side 2)
Native American
Lakota, Great Plains Region
c. 1880
wood, pigment
Florida Museum of Natural History

Figure 56 (right)
Pipe
Native American
Undetermined tribe, Eastern Woodlands Region
c. 1880
catlinite
Florida Museum of Natural History

61

Nicco and I continued reviewing the photographs of the pipe bowls and pipe stems (figures 54-56). I explained to Nicco these were of particular interest because I was very aware of the "Red Road," the use of the pipe, and the connection with the White Buffalo Calf Society. I had great concern about the exhibition of the pipe, since such pipes are still being used.

My first encounter with the "Red Road" was when Robert Stead, a North Dakota Sioux medicine man, arrived in Oakland, California, to conduct healing ceremonies to which everyone was welcome. The term "Red Road" refers to the way of life one follows when embracing the pipe. The ceremonies were held at night at the Intertribal Friendship House in Oakland, in the middle of the city. At first, attendance at the ceremonies was sparse but slowly results started happening.

Robert told the story of how the pipe came to the Sioux people. Of how it was a woman, White Buffalo Calf Woman, who brought the sacred pipe to the people. Of how he himself was chosen to carry the pipe, of stories of healing and that the pipe's main purpose is that of healing physically, spiritually, and mentally. At first, attendance was sparse, but slowly the number of people increased as members of different tribes, together with African Americans, whites, and Asians attended the ceremonies.

PART 4: FAITH

Nicco was enthusiastic as she talked about the life of sacred objects and how without the proper conditions the objects were just that—objects. We talked about collecting the sacred and the need to own. Why was it so important for anthropologists and collectors to own that which never could, in actuality, be theirs? The acquisition of spiritual, personal power through purchase is an amusing thought. As we talked, I thought about the power of the sacred within the individual. Nicco made a distinction concerning things and pieces, which are spiritually useless when separated from the conditions to make everything work. For instance, the pipes could only be activated when in the possession of the rightful owner. When not in possession, they are merely inert objects as opposed to objects that are alive and living.

We talked about NAGPRA, the Native American Graves and Repatriation Act of 1990 (Public Law No. 101-601).[10] How this legislation does not address the remains of certain Native peoples thereby preventing the return of certain sacred objects to Native peoples, and that there is much work left to be done as many tribes do not have the budgets to examine every collection. And about how some institutions have refused to relinquish remains without absolute proof. For example, the Phoebe Hearst Museum's Native Remains Collections would have included Ishi if it were not for Kroeber's intervention. The process for repatriation is very stringent, and at times proving individual or communal ownership is virtually impossible.

It is not surprising that Native spirituality is viewed as something in the past since, sadly, most of America has no real knowledge of contemporary Native life. There is a belief that the sacred songs, the way of life is gone. But the ceremonies are ongoing; faith is strong. In my travels I have witnessed the strength of Native spirituality. In upstate New York, for example, I have participated with the Haudenosaunee in the Strawberry Thanksgiving at the New Town Long House, and at the Allegheny Long House I have watched the young women sitting proud, singing loud and strong. Future clan mothers claiming song. "For an outsider, attending these ceremonies also means learning about attitudes, about codes of conduct—learning to be considerate of those who are there as participants-observers; learning to show respect by quiet unobtrusiveness, not asking questions of others during the ceremony, of behaving politely in general—behaving just as one would at any other ceremony. Some ceremonies are closed to outsiders, but many are open and at these all people are welcome. 'We don't mind outsiders or non-Indians coming to watch the dances,' says Joe Herrera of Chichiti Pueblo, 'because they are part of it. As long as they have that respect.'"[11]

Faith is strong in the Strawberry Thanksgiving dance at Point Reyes, the "Big Time" and "Bear Dance" of the Northern California tribes. Faith is present in the ceremonies of my father's people, on the Navajo Nation, Beauty Way, the winter Yei bii chee, the summer Squaw dances. In Hawai'i faith is danced and sung in the ancient hula and chants of genealogy. The Snake Dance of the Hopi, Thanksgiving dances of the Pueblos in New Mexico. My mother's people, the Seminole and Muskogee, the Green Corn dance. Faith is strong.

The evolution of ritual incorporated Christianity, including the translation of hymn books into Muskogee, so that Native religion could survive. Native spirituality surviving even at times when it had to go underground, surviving in spite of being outlawed by the federal government, surviving even in times when Native spirituality is appropriated, manipulated, translated, and sold for profit by New Age entrepreneurs. I believe that the rest of America has no idea of the fathomless faith of Native people. The rest of America has no idea of the intimate rituals that are being conducted at this very moment.

As Nicco and I were saying good-bye, I breathed a sigh of relief. By sharing information with me she had given me a sign of faith. I now knew I could take on without hesitation the responsibility for writing about the artifacts to be exhibited. The responsibility for letting people know Aboriginal religion is strong and for reminding everyone that the words "Vanishing" and "Disappearing" are merely English words.

Acknowledgments: An essay such as this could not be written alone. I would like to acknowledge Takashela for spiritual guidance; Nicco Strange Owl for valuable information; and Nathan Jackson, Moira Roth, Sara Ramirez, and Veronica Passalacqua for their input. Special thanks to Amalia Amaki for our conversation about faith.

Hulleah J. Tsinhnahjinnie
Photographer, writer

---

1. Paula Richardson Fleming and Judith Luskey, *The North American Indians in Early Photographs* (London: Phaidon, 1986) 140.
2. Oroville Register, Oroville, California, August 29, 1911.
3. Mary Ashe Miller, *San Francisco Call*, September 6, 1911.
4. Rebecca J. Dobkins, Carey T. Caldwell, and Frank R. Lapena, *Memory and Imagination: The Legacy of Maidu Indian Artist Frank Day* (Seattle: University of Washington Press, 1997.)
5. http://www.qal.berkeley.edu/hearst/history
6. Ibid.
7. Gerald Vizenor, "Ishi Bares His Chest: Tribal Simulations and Survivance." In *Partial Recall*, Lucy Lippard, ed. (New York: The New Press, 1992) 66.
8. Dee Alexander Brown, *Bury My Heart at Wounded Knee: An Indian History of the American West* (New York: Bantam Books, 1972) 415.
9. Ibid., 435.
10. See www.sfsu.edu/nagpra/welcome.htm for in-depth information.
11. Tryntje Van Ness Seymour, *When the Rainbow Touches Down.* (Phoenix: The Heard Museum, 1988) 5.

Figure 57
Icon of the Virgin and Child
Russia
c. 1900
wood, tempera, silver leaf
Lent by Gary Hollingsworth, Orlando, Florida

RITUAL OBJECTS AND PRIVATE DEVOTION

A Random Meditation

TRADITIONAL, SLIGHTLY SIMPLIFIED, AND PERHAPS TOO CATEGORICALLY RIGID WAYS OF CONSIDERING RELIGION HAVE TENDED TO SEPARATE BELIEFS FROM PRACTICES.

Beliefs are expressed in dogmas and are transmitted through words, at times only spoken ones, more frequently—and especially in the three revealed religions of Judaism, Christianity, and Islam—through written texts. Such books are sometimes believed to be revelations of divine origin, or they may be merely records of rules, holy narratives, or interpretations of holy texts.

Practices are exemplified by rituals. What are these rituals? In the few pages that follow I will sketch out, first, something of the moments in time and ways in which rituals are enacted and then offer a few remarks on the ritual objects which form the topic of this exhibition.

Rituals can be grandiose events held, usually, at fixed intervals and on prescribed dates. They may involve many thousands of participants, as happens with the *hajj*, the yearly Muslim pilgrimage to the holy cities Mecca and Medina in the Arabian peninsula, when nearly a million believers gather for a few days of intensely felt and carefully orchestrated actions. Similar, but on a much smaller scale, is the celebration of Easter in the Church of the Holy Sepulcher in Jerusalem, and in thousands of churches wherever Christians are found. This event, so central to Christianity, is recalled every year with special brilliance. The Jewish Passover also has a uniquely special quality in Jerusalem, where, since ancient times, Jews from many places gather, or at *seder* dinners to which family and friends are invited wherever there is a Jewish community. Such large-scale yearly events exist in many other religious systems, especially in those religions in which pilgrimages to hallowed places play a significant role. In many instances, the performance of the ritual requires a hierarchy of participants—clergy specially trained and anointed, or simply leaders appointed for prayers or other activities—masses of faithful believers, and a host of services, from the preparation of food to, in our own times, preparation for medical emergencies. This hierarchy is frequently expressed through differences in attire, or through signs and symbols. Bishops and priests wear crosses different from those worn by ordinary people. Turbans vary in shape, size, or color, depending on the learning or parentage of Muslim leaders. In today's world, armbands identify medical personnel, guards, or ushers needed for certain ceremonies, but other distinctive signs must have existed in the past, even if we are no longer able to recognize them. For the Muslim pilgrimage, a sort of uniform is created, as all the faithful wrap a white cloth around their bodies in carefully prescribed ways. This cloth is kept forever and is often used eventually as a shroud.

These grandiose ritual events can or should affect all the faithful of any one religion. But there are also smaller versions of these "universal" events which occur in many sanctuaries devoted to local or sectarian holy men and women or heroes. In some, usually rural or arid, parts of the world, these local sanctuaries are easily identifiable in the landscape. Ruined or still in use, they are often found on heights outside of inhabited areas, so they dominate the surroundings and their holiness can be seen from afar. These sanctuaries are usually places for local pilgrimages or for meeting very practical needs like curing the sick, helping to find a good spouse, or guaranteeing the birth of a son. Devotional objects may be connected with them and, sometimes, there are specific identifying signs, like the shell of St. James found on the medieval pilgrim routes to Compostela in northwestern Spain. Many such signs exist as well in the Shi'ite world of Iran with its many sanctuaries around the tombs of descendants of Ali, the son-in-law of the Prophet and first *imam* of the Shi'ite persuasion.

Usually, grandiose rituals like pilgrimages take place only once a year, although most systems of faith have accepted, even encouraged, private or small group pilgrimages at other times of the year; thus, the *'umra* is a sort of private pilgrimage for Muslims which does not earn all the merits of the *hajj* but which can be a very important and a very moving experience, as is true of similar occurrences in Christianity, Hinduism, or Judaism.

The most common religious practices of all faiths occur daily or weekly and tend to be restricted to local communities, even if the performances involved are more or less the same everywhere. Usually they have a collective component, as when the faithful gather in churches, mosques, synagogues, or temples and engage there, usually at specified times and, most often with the assistance of clergy, in ceremonies with carefully prescribed rules. Even if normally only attended on Sundays, Christian masses can be, and are in monasteries, daily repetitions of a highly thought out sequence of statements, proclamations, readings, and prayers culminating with the celebration of a mystery. Collective Muslim prayer in mosques is also a well-orchestrated ritual with a leader in front (the *imam*), a direction faced by everyone, and traditional gestures repeated by all. There are no special clothes for Muslim prayer, but the obligation of cleanliness has created a ritual for washing just before prayer. Readings from the Scripture and a sermon usually accompany Friday prayer. In synagogues as well, a weekly ritual combines prayers, recitations, sermons, and readings under the direction of a rabbi. Identifying signs are worn by some of the participants, and liturgical implements like the Torah or the *menorah* are visible in the building.

And then there are private rituals, expressions of piety or of belief which are engaged in not because of some collective or statutory obligation, but because of an individual's need to surround his or her life with signs of his or her faith. This level of ritual behavior can take many forms. It can be simply hanging an icon in the corner of a room and burning some oil in front of it (figure 57) as a sort of blessing over whatever happens in the house. It can be a prayer rug with which one travels and proclaims privately one's acceptance of the will of God (plates 13, 14). It can be strings of beads whose constant fingering accompanies the recitation of praises or of a prayer. It can be reading beautifully illuminated, at times even illustrated, holy books (figure 58). The Scriptures themselves, the Koran and various books of the Bible, received particular attention on the part of patrons and of artists. But many Scripture-derived books, liturgical manuals, prayer books (figure 59 and plate 1), legal texts, and interpretations were, occasionally, also illustrated or, at the very least, expensively decorated. Images in Christianity and words in Judaism and Islam were used on almost any imaginable article, practical objects like magic bowls or metal sculptures of extended hands warding one against the evil eye, commemorative objects like wedding rings, or simply decorative objects like the many wooden plaques found all over the Muslim world which bear the name of Allah, God, and are bought as souvenirs and used to decorate an office or a home.

Claude Lévi-Strauss wrote that a ritual "consists in words spoken, gestures accomplished, objects manipulated independently of any expressed exegesis."[1] And, from my own examples, it is possible, on the simplest level, to argue that, whatever the type of ritual, whether it is the grandiose and relatively rare one, the frequent and collective, or the private, all forms of ritual were accompanied by objects. There always were "things" connected with rituals. They are

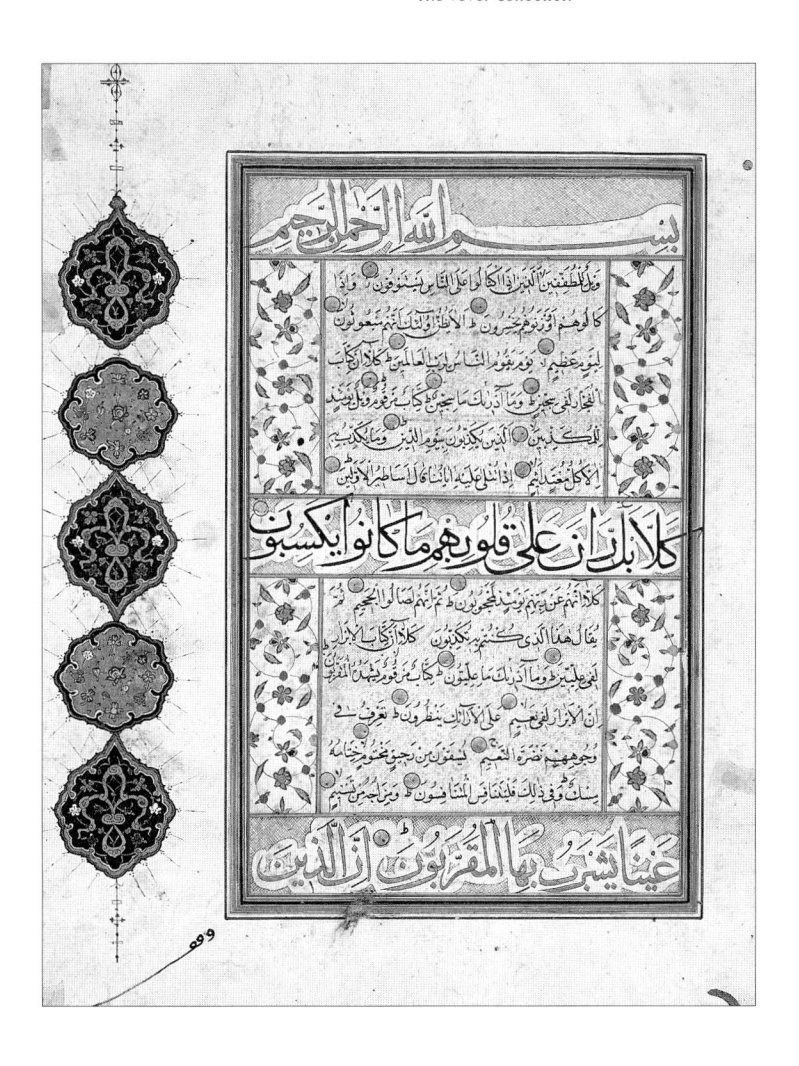

Figure 58
Folio from a Koran
Turkey
2nd half of 16th century
script: Muhaqqaq and Naskh
paper, opaque watercolor, ink, gold
Courtesy of the Arthur M. Sackler Gallery,
Smithsonian Institution, Washington, D.C.,
The Vever Collection

Figure 59
Folio from a Book of Prayers
Turkey
August-September, 1715
script: Naskh
paper, opaque watercolor, ink, gold
Courtesy of the Arthur M. Sackler Gallery,
Smithsonian Institution, Washington, D.C.,
The Vever Collection

made in practically every material known to mankind, and they can range from the great and unique works of world art (the *Ghent Altarpiece* or the *Sistine Chapel*) to crude and rough items manufactured by amateur artisans. Their immense variety not only reflects their aesthetic value and quality, it also involves what is being said on or by them.

Let us consider writing, the putting of inscriptions on the walls of buildings and on objects. In most mosques, schools of theology and law known as *madrasahs*, or other buildings dedicated by traditional Islamic piety to social purposes, there are usually very large and very visible inscriptions comprised of appropriate quotations from the Koran; the proclamation of God's unique and beneficent power (they all begin, "In the name of God, the Compassionate, the Merciful"); the identification of the patron and, at times, the builder or the artisans who worked on it; and finally, a date. This sort of inscription, for which there are equivalents in Christianity and Judaism, is a ritual object because it is repetitive, fairly consistent in structure, and evocative of the presence and blessing of the divine. Yet it lacks devotion, personal passion, or even feeling. By contrast, consider the thousands of graffiti which are scratched or painted on walls, rocks, and whatever other surface was available, all over the Muslim world. Their texts are also very similar to each other, with only minor modifications to the simple prayer "May God forgive me," and usually with the name of some now-forgotten human being. Hardly significant works of art, these humble and formulaic inscriptions are the only witnesses we possess to the private fears of unknown men, who, over the centuries, traveled, worked, were sick, and died alone and away from the place of their normal life. These inscriptions are indeed expressions of devotion. In the Christian world, this same private devotion expresses itself in thousands of churches through the innumerable *ex-votos* asking God to cure sickness or to prevent the onslaught of pestilence. It is also evident in small items, statues, or gifts found in churches and cemeteries. And it is difficult not to be moved by the many candles which are lit anonymously in front of altars, each of which reflects someone's prayer, wish, or memory. Like the prophylacteries of Orthodox Jews and the myriad amulets found in all religions, they are the remaining traces of human needs and emotions that appear standardized to us today, but that are in fact highly personal testimonies to intimate feelings.

Somewhere in between the beautiful formal writing on major architectural monuments and the private anguish of graffiti lie what may be called the instruments of hope and fear as well as of canonical obligations. Such are the magic bowls with, usually, a simple grid whose slots are filled with letters or numbers. Specialists known as geomancers knew how to connect these letters in order to forecast the future or help with the present. Many of these bowls reflect a peculiar world of belief which is only partly attached to organized religion, but which all religions sought to harness through the imagery and the writing on the objects. Wedding rings acquire Christian symbols and, in fact, nearly all aspects of life are given forms relating them to a faith. These forms can be practical, as with Muslim prayer rugs which allow any believer to create, more or less at will, his own restricted space for prayer. When traveling in Muslim lands, it is often very moving to see, at appropriate times, policemen or custom officials make a personal space alongside a busy road or inside an office building in order to prostrate themselves toward God. It is even more profound to witness, as I did many years ago in the Syrian desert, a simple and illiterate elderly nomad, without family or known tribal attachment, make himself a *mihrab* (the niche indicating the direction of prayer toward Mecca) of stones (whose direction he would occasionally change) and, just before sunrise, ask in a loud voice God's forgiveness and God's favor. What his sins were, we never learned, but the simple stones he laid out on the arid earth were necessary for him to express some fundamental human fear of life to come.

These random observations, recollections, and remarks do not easily lend themselves to conclusions. Yet they allow me to develop two broad thoughts for the appreciation of the exhibition. One, noted by nearly all writers, mostly anthropologists, on ritual and devotion, is that the edges between practices and beliefs are always blurred. Superstitions and universal psychological and emotional needs reflect beliefs or are manipulated by practices derived from beliefs. The instruments of this relationship are often objects, at times made under the direction of official authority and endowed with high aesthetic and technical values, at other times by artisans for a pious market, or even by amateurs for a specific personal purpose. Thus, a merchant in Herat (today in northwestern Afghanistan) made, in the middle of the twelfth century, a pen case of bronze inlaid with silver, a perfectly useful object in any literate society. He made it to give to his brother, who was going to Mecca for the pilgrimage, a round trip that could easily take two years without any possibility of communication between the time of departure and the return and from which many pilgrims never came back. In the inscription with which he decorated the object, the merchant recorded enough information to reconstruct his purposes. The pen case is preserved in the Hermitage Museum in St. Petersburg, Russia, and is obviously a striking gesture of fraternal affection, but it is remarkable because it illustrates how a personal history can transform almost any object into an object of devotion.[2]

The pen case is from the Islamic Middle Ages, but Christianity and Judaism can probably furnish many comparable examples. And it is in the light of this sort of experience, in which private feelings and revealed faith operate together, if not always very clearly, that many objects in the exhibition should probably be understood. We will never know their full story, even when they are close to us in time and in the place of their manufacture and use, but we can imagine that story and, even if we have to invent it, we may not always be off the mark.

The second thought that can be derived from these remarks is of a more general type. In a perceptive essay on fact and law, Clifford Geertz wrote of the styles and meanings projected by certain key legal terms that "they do not just regulate behavior, they construe it."[3] The point could be extended to objects of piety and devotion, magical bowls, prayer rugs, prophylacteries, or icons. Whatever their origin, at some point they begin to control and to shape behavior. Therein lies their fascination and their magic. They do it according to clearly established sets of rules, just like all the games played by man. But, in games, however strict the rules may be, there is always a winner whose identity is unknown when the game begins. In rituals and in liturgical ceremonies, there are also rules, but the outcome is always known. The rules do not serve to challenge any individual's talents and capacities but to guarantee success and salvation. Many objects once removed from the specificity of the reasons for their creation have lost some of their ritual certainty but have acquired the power to fire the imagination of those who observe them. They are no longer parts of a spectacle, even if this had been their early role, but they can lead us to the real lives of men and women in the past or elsewhere and thereby enrich our own.

Oleg Grabar
Professor Emeritus
School of Historical Studies
Institute for Advanced Study
Princeton, New Jersey

---

1 Edmund Leach, "Ritual," in *International Encyclopedia of the Social Sciences*, David L. Sills, ed., vol. 13 (New York, 1968) 521-522.
2 L.T. Giuzalian, "The bronze pen-case of 542/1148 in the Hermitage," *Ars Orientalis* 7 (1968): 95-119.
3 Clifford Geertz, *Local Knowledge* (New York: Basic Books, 1983) 215.

SELECTED BIBLIOGRAPHY

Arthur M. Sackler Gallery. *Puja: Expressions of Hindu Devotion.* Washington, D.C.: Smithsonian Institution, 1996 (video tape).

Bechert, Heinz, and Richard Gombrich, eds. *The World of Buddhism.* London: Thames and Hudson, 1984.

Ben-Amos, Paula Girshick. *The Art of Benin.* London: British Museum Press, 1995.

Berman, Lawrence M. *Catalogue of Egyptian Art.* Cleveland, Ohio: The Cleveland Museum of Art, 1999.

Bothmer, Dietrich von, ed. *Glories of the Past: Ancient Art from the Shelby White and Leon Levy Collection.* New York: The Metropolitan Museum of Art, 1990.

Bourgeois, Arthur P. *Art of the Yaka and Suku.* Meudon, France: A. & F. Chaffin, 1984.

Brown, Dee Alexander. *Bury My Heart at Wounded Knee: An Indian History of the American West.* New York: Bantam Books, 1972.

Burkert, Walter (translated by John Raffian). *Greek Religion.* Cambridge: Harvard University Press, 1985.

Chaffin, Alain. *L'art Kota: Les Figures de Reliquaire.* Meudon, France: A. & F. Chaffin, 1979.

Cole, Herbert M., and Chike C. Aniakor. *Igbo Arts: Community and Cosmos.* Los Angeles: Museum of Cultural History, University of California, 1984.

Cole, Herbert M., and Doran H. Ross. *The Arts of Ghana.* Los Angeles: Museum of Cultural History, University of California, 1977.

Drewal, Henry John, John Pemberton, 3rd, and Rowland Abiodun. *Yoruba: Nine Centuries of African Art and Thought.* Allen Wardwell, ed. New York: Center for African Art and H. N. Abrams, 1989.

Eliade, Mircea (translated by Willard R. Trask). *The Sacred and the Profane: The Nature of Religion.* New York: Harcourt, Brace, 1959.

Ettinghausen, Richard. *Prayer Rugs.* Washington, D.C.: Textile Museum, 1974.

Fleming, Paula Richardson, and Judith Luskey. *The North American Indians in Early Photographs.* London: Phaidon, 1986.

Frankfort, Henry. *The Art and Architecture of the Ancient Orient.* New Haven, Connecticut: Yale University Press, 1996.

Gavin, Robin Farwell. *Traditional Arts of Spanish New Mexico.* Sante Fe: Museum of New Mexico Press, 1994.

Geertz, Clifford. *Local Knowledge: Further Essays in Interpretive Anthropology.* New York: Basic Books, 1983.

Grossman, Grace Cohen. *Jewish Art.* New York: Hugh Lauter Levin Associates, Inc., 1995.

Huntington, Susan L., and John C. Huntington. *Leaves from the Bodhi Tree: The Art of Pala India (8th-12th Centuries) and Its International Legacy.* Dayton, Ohio: Dayton Art Institute and the University of Washington Press, 1989.

Ishida, Mosaku, et al. (translated by Charles S. Terry). *Japanese Buddhist Prints.* Tokyo and Palo Alto: Kodansha International, 1963.

Kozloff, Arielle P., David Gordon Mitten, et al. *The Gods Delight: The Human Figure in Classical Bronze.* Cleveland, Ohio: The Cleveland Museum of Art, 1988.

Levi-Strauss, Claude (translated by Claire Jacobson and Brooke Grundfest Schoepf). *Structural Anthropology.* New York: Basic Books, 1963.

Loughran, Katheryne S. *Somalia in Word and Image.* Washington, D.C.: Foundation for Cross Cultural Understanding and Indiana University Press, 1986.

MacGaffey, Wyatt. *Astonishment and Power.* Washington, D.C.: Smithsonian Institution Press for the National Museum of African Art, 1993.

Phillips, Ruth B. *Representing Woman: Sande Masquerades of the Mende of Sierra Leone.* Los Angeles, California: UCLA Fowler Museum of Cultural History, 1995.

Poynor, Robin. *African Art at the Harn Museum: Spirit Eyes, Human Hands.* Gainesville: University Press of Florida, 1995.

Snellgrove, David, ed. *The Image of the Buddha.* Paris and Tokyo: Kodansha International/UNESCO, 1978.

Vizenor, Gerald. *Ishi Bares His Chest: Tribal Simulations and Survivance.* In Lucy Lippard, ed., *Partial Recall.* New York: The New Press, 1992.

Wieck, Roger S. *Painted Prayers, The Book of Hours in Medieval and Renaissance Art.* New York: George Braziller, Inc., and The Pierpont Morgan Library, 1997.

Zwarf, Z. *Buddhism: Art and Faith.* London: The British Museum and The British Library, 1985.

Figure 60
Stephen Antonakos
American, b. Laconia, Greece, 1926
Wall Cross with Votive Candle
1995
wood, glass, wax candle
Lent by Stephen Antonakos

CHECKLIST OF THE EXHIBITION

Dimensions are given in inches, height preceding width preceding depth

ANTIQUITY

Statuette of a Standing Worshiper
Mesopotamia or Syria
c. 2400 B.C.E.
limestone
6 7/16
Lent by Shelby White and Leon Levy
W/L 222

Female Statuette
Crete, Minoan
c. 1600-1450 B.C.E.
bronze
2 5/8
Courtesy of the Arthur M. Sackler Museum
Harvard University Art Museums
David M. Robinson Fund and Gift of Mr. and Mrs. Edwin L. Weisl, Jr.
1975.60

Domestic Shrine
Egypt, Thebes
New Kingdom, Dynasty 18
Reign of Tuthmosis III
(c. 1479-1425 B.C.E.)
limestone
16 4/5
The Cleveland Museum of Art
Gift of the John Huntington Art and Polytechnic Trust
1920.2002

Statuette of a Horse
Greece
8th century B.C.E.
bronze
4 3/5
The Cleveland Museum of Art
John L. Severance Fund
1998.173

Ram Bearer (Kriophoros)
Greece, Crete
7th century B.C.E.
terra cotta, polychromy
7 x 3 7/8
The Cleveland Museum of Art
John L. Severance Fund
1998.172

Statuette of a Nude Youth (Kouros)
Probably from Magna Graecia
Archaic, c. 480-470 B.C.E.
bronze, copper
10 1/2
Lent by Shelby White and Leon Levy
W/L 498

Statuette of a Worshiper
Roman, Early Imperial
1st half of the 1st century C.E.
bronze, silver
Inscribed on the right leg: ΠΟΥΒΛΙΣ ΑΧΑΕΙΚΟΣ ΕΙΞΑΜΕΝΟΙ ΑΝΕΘΗΚΑΝ:
"Publi[o]s Achaiikos, having vowed, dedicated [this]."
8 5/8
Lent by Shelby White and Leon Levy
W/L 215

Four funerary sculptures of the family of Vibia Drosis

Stele of Gaius Vibius Felix
Roman, Early Flavian
c. 69-80
marble
Inscribed (on the front): To Gaius Vibius Felix [who] lived 49 years, made by Vibia Drosis [for] her dearest father; (on the left side): QVIS/QVIS/ HVIC/MONI[sic]/ MENTO/ CONTI/MELIA/ NONFEC/ERIT/DOLORI/ NVIVMEX/PERICA/TVR [in a less careful cursive script, as the spelling errors confirm, than the inscription on the front].
33
Lent by Shelby White and Leon Levy
W/L 235.1

Stele of Gaius Vibius Severus
Roman, Early Flavian
c. 69-80
Inscribed (on the front): To Gaius Vibius Severus, who lived [for] 23 years; made by Vibia Drosis for her dearest son.
29 1/2
Lent by Shelby White and Leon Levy
W/L 235.3

Stele of Vibia Drosis
Roman, Early Flavian
c. 69-80
marble
Inscribed (on the front): Vibia Drosis made this for herself and her descendants: (on the right side): HIC/AMOR/FIDES/ PIETAS/EST.
36 5/16
Lent by Shelby White and Leon Levy
W/L 235.2

Cinerary Urn of Gaius Vibius Herostratus
Roman, Early Flavian
c. 85-95
marble
Inscribed (on the front): C. VIBIVS/ HEROSTRATVS/VIBIA/ .C./L/HAERESIS; the sides bear incised circles.
13 1/4
Lent by Shelby White and Leon Levy
W/L 235.4

Isis Lactans Figurine
Palestine, Jerusalem
4th-5th century
molded terra cotta
4 7/8
University of Pennsylvania Museum of Archaeology and Anthropology, Philadelphia
29-103-935

BUDDHIST

Miniature Votive Stupa
China, Gansu Province
Northern Liang Period (397-460)
dated 435
steatite
6 5/8
The Cleveland Museum of Art
Purchase from the J. H. Wade Fund
1990.84

Shakyamuni Preaching: A Votive Stele
China
Northern Zhou Dynasty (557-581)
c. 565
yellow mottled stone
5 3/8 x 3 7/8
The Cleveland Museum of Art
Gift of the John Huntington Art and Polytechnic Trust
1915.561

Standing Bodhisattva
China
Sui Dynasty (581-618)
6th century
gilt bronze
4 1/2
The Cleveland Museum of Art
The Severance and Greta Millikin Purchase Fund
1979.20

Bodhisattva Guanyin
China
Tang Dynasty (618-907)
7th-8th century
gilt bronze
4 5/8 x 2 1/16
Asian Art Museum of San Francisco
Gift of Mr. and Mrs. Alexander D. Calhoun, Jr.
B73 S19

Miniature Pagoda Containing a Printed Dharani Charm
Japan
c. 764-770
wood, gesso
8 3/4
Courtesy, Peabody Essex Museum, Salem, MA
E19318

Stupa Reliquary
China
Tang Dynasty (618-907)
silvered bronze
6 3/8 x 3 5/8 x 3 5/8
Harn Museum of Art Collection
Museum purchase, gift of Dr. and Mrs. David A. Cofrin
1999.16

Banner Painting of Standing Guanyin Attended by Two Donors
China
Tang Dynasty (618-907) to Five Dynasties Period (907-960)
c. 9th-10th century
38 x 24 3/4
Courtesy of the Arthur M. Sackler Museum
Harvard University Art Museums
First Fogg Expedition to China,1923-1924
1925.12

Seated Buddha
Indonesia, Java
9th century
bronze
6 3/4 x 3 3/8
Asian Art Museum of San Francisco
Gift of the Lyda Ebert Foundation
1988.21

Miniature Stupa with Illustrations of Jataka Tales
China
Five Dynasties Period (907-960)
dated 955
bronze
5 1/4 x 3 1/4 x 3 3/8
Courtesy of the Arthur M. Sackler Museum
Harvard University Art Museums
Gift of Nasli M. Heeramaneck
1930.105

Shakyamuni
Korea
Koryo Period
(918-1392)
wood, traces of black lacquer
17
The Cleveland Museum of Art
John L. Severance Fund
1988.152

Votive Plaque Depicting Buddha in Bhumisparsa Mudra
Burma
11th century
molded terra cotta
5 3/8 x 3 7/8
Courtesy of the Arthur M. Sackler Museum Harvard University Art Museums
Louis Sidney Thierry Memorial Fund
1981.34

Eleven-headed Kannon
Japan
late Heian (794-1185)-early Kamakura Period (1185-1333)
12th century
bronze
6 1/2 x 3 3/4
The Cleveland Museum of Art
Gift of Mrs. John Lyon Collyer in memory of her mother,
Mrs. G. M. G. Forman
1960.279

Head of Buddha
Thailand, Hariphunchai
12th-13th century
bronze repoussé
6 1/2 x 3 7/8
Asian Art Museum of San Francisco
Gift of Ed Nagel
B73 B17

Bodhisattva Avalokiteshvara
Nepal
13th century
gilt bronze, semi-precious stones
4 3/4 x 4 x 2 5/8
Harn Museum of Art Collection
Museum purchase, gift of Michael A. Singer
1997.22

Prajnaparamita
Central Tibet
13th-14th century
copper alloy with copper and silver inlay, semi-precious stones, traces of paint
3 3/8 x 2 1/4 x 1 3/4
Virginia Museum of Fine Arts, Richmond
The Berthe and John Ford Collection, Gift of Berthe and John Ford
91.521

Shōtoku Taishi as a Child
Japan
Kamakura Period (1185-1333)
early 14th century
joined wood, black lacquer, traces of color, crystal
27
The Cleveland Museum of Art
Gift of Mr. and Mrs. James Campbell Weir in memory of
Dr. and Mrs. William Hawksley Weir
1989.76

Stupa Reliquary
Tibet
13th-17th century
copper alloy
9 3/8 x 4 1/2
Virginia Museum of Fine Arts, Richmond
The Arthur and Margaret Glasgow Fund and
The Asiatic Art Acquisition Fund
92.165

Dharma Master rDo rje seng ge
Tibetan (1152-1220)
Book Cover with Buddhist Deities
Nepal or Tibet
c. 15th century
wood, polychromy, gilt
10 5/8 x 28
Courtesy of the Arthur M. Sackler Museum Harvard University Art Museums
The Hofer Collection of the Arts of Asia
1978.515

Votive Plaque (tsha-tsha)
Tibet
c. 15th century
molded terra cotta
6 1/16 x 4 1/4 x 1 3/8
Harn Museum of Art Collection
Museum purchase, gift of Ruth Pruitt Phillips
1997.24

Konoe Nobutada
Japanese (1565-1614)
Kitano Tenjin
Momoyama Period (1573-1615)
ink on paper
36 1/2 x 18 3/8
Private collection, Cambridge, Massachusetts

Amulet Worn by Shugendo Practitioner
Japan
Edo Period (1615-1868)
woodblock print on paper
3 x 423
Private collection, Cambridge, Massachusetts

Hakuin Ekaku
Japanese (1685-1769)
Calligraphy with the Posthumous Name of Prince Shōtoku
Edo Period (1615-1868), 18th century
ink on paper
38 3/4 x 10 3/4
Private collection, Cambridge, Massachusetts

Pilgrim's Bell
Japan
Edo Period (1615-1868)
silver, wood
2 1/4 x 10 1/4
Courtesy, Peabody Essex Museum, Salem, MA
1913 E15, 590

Pilgrim's Miniature Gong and Striker
Japan
Edo Period (1615-1868)
bronze, brass
9 1/4
Courtesy, Peabody Essex Museum, Salem, MA
E15, 725

Print for Pilgrims
Japan
Edo Period (1615-1868)
woodblock print on paper
21 1/2 x 8 1/2
Lent by Drs. Geoffrey and Ming-mei Redmond

Ga'u
Tibet
18th century
brass, silver, clay, polychromy, cowrie shells, bells, cloth
7 3/8 x 6 3/8 x 3
Harn Museum of Art Collection
Museum purchase, funds provided by museum visitors
1998.22

Lama, Yongs-'dzin-ngag-dbang bzang-po
Tibet
18th century
gilt bronze, turquoise, silver
7 1/4 x 4 1/8 x 3 1/2
Asian Art Museum of San Francisco
Gift of Raymond G. and Milla L. Handley
B86 B8

Miniature Shrine in the Form of a Lotus Petal
Japan, Edo Period (1615-1868)
late 18th-early 19th century
sandalwood, polychromy, gilt
3 x 2 1/4
Courtesy of the Arthur M. Sackler Museum Harvard University Art Museums
Gift of Dorothy A. Heath and Milan A. Heath, Jr.,
class of 1959, in honor of John M. Rosenfield
1999.122 a, b

Prayer Beads
Nepal or Tibet
late 19th-early 20th century
glass, seeds, stone, copper alloy, fiber
dimensions indeterminate
Lent by Ginger and Dave Bross

Prayer Beads
China
late 19th-early 20th century
carved seeds, string
8 15/16 (including tassel)
Wexner Center for the Arts, The Ohio State University
The Dr. Bliss M. and Mildred A. Wiant Collection of Chinese Art
1978.431

Votive Plaque (tsha-tsha) Six-arm Mahakala Stepping on Ganesha
United States, San Francisco
1989
clay
2 3/4 x 2 1/2
Tibetan mold from Beijing, China
bronze
3 1/4 x 2 15/16
Qinxuan Collection

Votive Plaque Amitayus, White Tara, and Ushnishavijaya
Mongolia, Ulaanbaatar
20th century
clay
1 7/8 x 1 3/4
Qinxuan Collection

Votive Plaque Dorje Legspa Riding on Ram, Holding Hammer and Bellows
Mongolia, Ulaanbaatar
20th century
clay
2 1/2 x 1 3/4
Qinxuan Collection

Votive Plaque Tsongkapa, Founder of the Gelug Sect
Mongolia
20th century
clay
1 1/2 x 1
Qinxuan Collection

Votive Plaque Bodhi-Leaf-Shaped Amulet with Seated Buddha
Thailand, Bangkok
possibly 20th century
clay
15/16 x 2/3
Qinxuan Collection

Votive Plaque (tsha-tsha) Amitayus, Seated, Holding Vase
Tibet
date unknown
clay
1 3/4
Qinxuan Collection

Votive Plaque (tsha-tsha) Amitayus, White Tara, and Ushnishavijaya
Tibet
date unknown
clay
2 3/4 x 2 1/3
Qinxuan Collection

Votive Plaque Akshobhya, Holding Dorje, Seated on Elephant Throne
Purchased in Beijing, China
date unknown
clay
2 3/4 x 2 1/4
Qinxuan Collection

Votive Plaque (tsha-tsha) Manjushri, Seated on Lion, Sword and Book on Lotuses
Tibet, Tashilhunpo
date unknown
clay
1 1/2 x 1 3/4
Qinxuan Collection

Votive Plaque Vaishravana, Seated on Lion, Holding Umbrella and Mongoose
Purchased in Beijing, China
date unknown
clay
1 3/4
Qinxuan Collection

Votive Plaque Vajrabhairava
China, Acquired in Beijing
date unknown
clay
1 1/2 x 1 1/3
Qinxuan Collection

HINDU

Durga Slaying the Buffalo Demon
India, Uttar Pradesh, Mathura
5th-6th century
red mottled sandstone
5 3/4 x 4 x 2
Harn Museum of Art Collection
Museum purchase, gift of Michael A. Singer
1998.23

Votive Lingam
India, Bengal
c. 20th century
blackened steatite
2 15/16 x 2 3/8 x 1 13/16
Harn Museum of Art Collection
Gift of Mr. and Mrs. Thomas J. Needham
1990.8.7

Krishna as the Dancing Butter Thief
Southern India, Madurai area(?)
c. late 17th century
bronze
5 3/4 x 3 7/16 x 2 1/8
Harn Museum of Art Collection
Gift of George P. Bickford
S-70-54

Bhu-Devi
Southern India, Madurai area
c. 1590
bronze
5 13/16 x 2 1/8 x 2
Harn Museum of Art Collection
Gift of George P. Bickford
S-66-15

Shaiva Saint
Southern India, Tamil Nadu
c. 17th century
bronze
4 x 3 1/16 x 2 1/8
Harn Museum of Art Collection
Gift of George P. Bickford
S-76-16

Krishna Playing the Flute and Dancing the Rasamandala with the Milkmaids
Southern India
17th-18th century
bronze
7 3/4 x 6 1/8 x 2 5/16
Asian Art Museum of San Francisco
The Avery Brundage Collection
B77 B5

Miniature Shrine (Shiva's Lingam)
India
17th-18th century
gilt silver
3 1/4 x 3 3/4
Asian Art Museum of San Francisco
The Avery Brundage Collection
B62 M68

JAIN

Digambara Jaina Shrine of the Tirthankara Chandra-Prabha
India, Northern Deccan, Chalukya(?)
c. 905
bronze
4 x 2 9/16 x 1 15/16
Harn Museum of Art Collection
Gift of George P. Bickford
S-75-74

Digambara Jaina Shrine of the Tirthankara Rsabanatha
India, Northern Karnatika, Kolhapur (?), Chalukya(?)
c. 11th or 12th century
bronze
8 1/2 x 5 1/8 x 4
Harn Museum of Art Collection
Gift of George P. Bickford
S-71-53

SHINTO

Kamidana, Household Shrine (dedicated to Ebisu)
Japan
Meiji Period (1868-1912)
wood, metal, paper, pigment
30 3/4 x 34 3/8 x 8 1/2
Courtesy, Peabody Essex Museum, Salem, MA
1985 E74, 020

O-fuda (Talisman) from Shinto Shrine
Japan
Meiji Period (1868-1912)
pigment on paper
6 3/4 x 3 3/4
Courtesy, Peabody Essex Museum, Salem, MA
E11635

INDIGENOUS AFRICAN

Ancestral Head (uhumwelao)
Nigeria, Benin, Edo People
terra cotta
11 x 8 1/2 x 7 1/4
Harn Museum of Art Collection
Gift of Rod McGalliard
1993.12.46

Commemorative Vessel (abusua kuruwa)
Ghana, Akan People
terra cotta
15 1/4 x 10 1/8 x 10 3/16
Harn Museum of Art Collection
Gift of Rod McGalliard
1993.12.26

Fertility Figure (akua'ba)
Ghana, Akan People (Asante)
wood, wire, beads
8 7/8 x 3 1/2 x 2 5/8
Harn Museum of Art Collection
Gift of Rod McGalliard
1990.14.53

Male Twin Statuettes (ere ibeji)
Nigeria, Yoruba People
wood, beads, leather, camwood patina
10 7/8 x 3 1/3 x 3 and
10 9/16 x 3 3/8 x 2 5/8
Harn Museum of Art Collection
Gift of Rod McGalliard
1993.12.3 and 4

Miniature Mask (gikhokho)
Democratic Republic of Congo, Pende People
ivory
2 1/2 x 1 x 1/2
Harn Museum of Art Collection
Gift of Rod McGalliard
1991.27.33

Personal Shrine for a Man (ikenga)
Nigeria, Ahoada area, Igbo People
wood, fiber, patina
8 x 2 x 2 5/8
Harn Museum of Art Collection
Gift of the Center for African Studies, University of Florida
S-77-14

Power Figure (nkisi, phuungu)
Democratic Republic of Congo, Yaka People
wood, cloth, feathers
8 x 2 1/2 x 1 1/2
Harn Museum of Art Collection
Gift of Dr. and Mrs. Saul A. Geronemus
S-72-37

Power Figure (nkisi, phuungu)
Democratic Republic of Congo, Yaka People
wood, cloth
7 1/2 x 3 1/8 x 2 1/8
Harn Museum of Art Collection
Gift of Rod McGalliard
1995.28.65

Reliquary Figure (mbulu)
Southeastern Gabon, Kota People
wood, brass, copper
13 3/8 x 6 1/4 x 1 7/8
Harn Museum of Art Collection
Museum purchase, funds provided by Michael A. Singer
1998.20

Sande Society Helmet Mask (zogbe)
Sierra Leone, Gola People
wood, metal
14 x 7 1/2 x 9
Harn Museum of Art Collection
Gift of Rod McGalliard
1990.14.97

Seated Female Figure (Esi Mansa)
Ghana, Akan People (Fante)
wood, paint, patina
18 x 5 1/2 x 5 1/2
Harn Museum of Art Collection
Gift of Rod McGalliard
1991.27.32

Shango Staff (oshe Shango)
Nigeria, Yoruba People
wood, patina
8 1/4 x 2 1/2 x 2
Harn Museum of Art Collection
Gift of the Center for African Studies, University of Florida
S-77-4

Spirit Spouse (blolo bla)
Ivory Coast, Baule People
wood, enamel
16 x 5 x 4 1/2
Harn Museum of Art Collection
Gift of Rod McGalliard
1990.14.118

NATIVE AMERICAN

Tobacco Pipe Pouch
Native American
Lakota, Great Plains Region
c. 1900
buckskin, seed beads, cotton thread, porcupine quills, aniline dyes
39 x 7 1/2
Florida Museum of Natural History
P-257

Ghost Dance Shirt
Native American
Lakota, Great Plains Region
c. 1890
cloth, polychromy, eagle feathers
34 x 19 1/2
Florida Museum of Natural History
P-66

Pipe Stem
Native American
Menominee, Eastern Woodlands Region
c. 1880
wood, pigment
2 1/4 x 23 3/4 x 2 1/4
Florida Museum of Natural History
P-185

Pipe Stem
Native American
Lakota, Great Plains Region
c. 1880
wood, pigment
19 1/8
Florida Museum of Natural History
P-204

Pipe
Native American
Lakota, Great Plains Region
c. 1880
catlinite, lead
7 3/8 x 3 5/8 x 1 1/8
Florida Museum of Natural History
92050

Pipe
Native American
Undetermined tribe, Eastern Woodlands Region
c. 1880
catlinite
2 1/2 4 1/4
Florida Museum of Natural History
P-2432

Pipe
Native American
Mississippian Culture, Eastern Woodlands Region
c. 15th-16th century
pottery
5 x 4 1/4 x 3 1/2
Florida Museum of Natural History
P-391

Koshari Katsina Doll (Hano Clown)
Native American
First Mesa, Hopi, Southwest Region
c. 1880-1890
cottonwood root, pigments
9 5/8 x 3 1/4 x 2
Florida Museum of Natural History
P-1922

Koyemsi Katsina Doll (Mud Head)
Native American
First Mesa, Hopi, Southwest Region
c. 1880-1890
cottonwood root, pigments
8 1/4 x 2 3/4 x 2
Florida Museum of Natural History
P-1924

Heheya Katsina Doll (Farmer)
Native American
First Mesa, Hopi, Southwest Region
c. 1880-1890
cottonwood root, pigments
9 1/4 x 5 x 3
Florida Museum of Natural History
P-1926

Kachin-mana Katsina Doll (Katsina Maiden)
Native American
First Mesa, Hopi, Southwest Region
c. 1880-1890
cottonwood root, pigments
9 x 4 1/4 x 2
Florida Museum of Natural History
P-1930

Umbilical Amulet in Shape of a Horny Toad
Native American
Lakota, Great Plains Region
c. 1880
buckskin, seed beads, cotton thread, sweetgrass, tin
1 x 5 x 3
Florida Museum of Natural History
26373

Umbilical Amulet in Shape of a Lizard
Native American
Crow, Great Plains Region
c. 1910
buckskin, seed beads, cotton thread, sweet grass, tin, horsehair, muslin
3/4 x 10 1/2 x 5
Florida Museum of Natural History
P105B

JEWISH

Haggadah
Holland, Amsterdam
1712
black ink on paper with copper-plate engravings
13 x 8
George A. Smathers Libraries, Special Collections and Area Studies
BM 675.P4 A56 1712

Gabriel Syren
German
Passover Plate
after 1727
pewter
15 1/4
The Jewish Museum, New York
Gift of Dr. Harry G. Friedman
F 2652

Otto Knoop
Dutch, Amsterdam
Hanging Sabbath Lamp
1740
silver
34
The Jewish Museum, New York
Gift of Dr. Harry G. Friedman
F 2257

Prayer Book Cover
Germany
c. 1750
silver
5 x 3 1/4
The Jewish Museum, New York
Gift of Dr. Harry G. Friedman
F 4208

Amulet and Case
Italy, Venice
18th century
silver, parchment
4 15/16 x 3 3/4
The Jewish Museum, New York
Gift of Dr. Harry G. Friedman
F 2082

Spice Container
Central Europe
late 18th century
silver
15 3/16
The Jewish Museum, New York
Gift of Lucille and Samuel Lemberg
JM 74-52

Hanukkah Lamp
Poland
18th-19th century
brass
11 7/8 x 10
The Jewish Museum, New York
Gift of Dr. Harry G. Friedman
F 2664

Passover Goblet
Bohemia
1845-1865
glass
8 1/2 x 3 1/2
The Jewish Museum, New York
Gift of Dr. Harry G. Friedman
F 4907

Lazarus Posen Witwe
German, Frankfurt
Traveling Hanukkah Lamp
1888-1911
silver
11/16 x 4 5/16 x 1 3/4 (closed)
The Jewish Museum, New York
Gift of Dr. Harry G. Friedman
F 2387

A. Riedel
Polish
Pair of Sabbath Candlesticks
Warsaw, 1890
silver
15 1/4
The Jewish Museum, New York
Gift in Memory of Bertha Flaxer, presented by her family
JM 7-51a, b

J. Rozencweig
Polish, Cracow
Pair of Tefillin Cases
19th century
silver
2 1/4 x 2 1/2
The Jewish Museum, New York
Benjamin and Rose Mintz Collection, Seminary Purchase, 1947
M 248 a, b

Kiddush Cup with Scroll Handle
Turkey
late 19th century
silver
2 3/16 x 2
The Jewish Museum, New York
Gift of Dr. Harry G. Friedman
F 1125

Jehuda Wolpert
American, b. Germany (1900-1981)
Mezuzah and Case
made in Jerusalem, c. 1950
silver, parchment, ink
3 11/16
The Jewish Museum, New York
Gift of Dr. Harry G. Friedman
U 8035

Moshe Zabari
American, New York
Memorial Lamp
1967
brass
3 1/4 x 4 x 1 5/8
The Jewish Museum, New York
Gift of the Albert A. List Family
JM 207-67

CHRISTIAN

Griffin Lamp
Early Byzantine
4th-6th century
copper alloy
7 x 8 1/2 x 2 1/2
Virginia Museum of Fine Arts, Richmond
The Arthur and Margaret Glasgow Fund
1966.10

Enkolpion with Dormition of the Virgin
Byzantine
c. 7th century
gold, crystal
enkolpion, 1 1/2 x 1; chain, 20
Virginia Museum of Fine Arts, Richmond
The Arthur and Margaret Glasgow Fund
67.29

Reliquary Cross
Byzantine
10th-12th century
gilt silver
3 3/4 x 1 5/8 x 5/16
Harn Museum of Art Collection
Museum purchase, gift of Michael A. Singer
1998.12

Crucifixion Panel (from diptych)
Northern France
14th century
ivory
4 3/4 x 2 5/8
Vanderbilt University Fine Arts Gallery
Gift of Mrs. Thomas Matthews
1975.004

School of the Boucicault Master
Leaf from a Book of Hours
France, Paris
1405-1420
vellum, gold leaf, tempera
3 1/8 x 4 1/4
Harn Museum of Art Collection
University Gallery purchase
M-74-76

Style of the Boucicault Master
Leaf from a Book of Hours
France, Paris
c. 1420
vellum, ink, tempera, gold
6 3/4 x 4 3/4
Lent by David and Hazel Stanley

Leaf from a Prayer Book
Holland
early 15th century
vellum, ink, tempera, gold
5 1/4 x 3 7/8
Harn Museum of Art Collection
University Gallery purchase
M-74-77

Two Leaves from a Book of Hours
Northern Italy, perhaps Bologna or Florence
c. 1440
vellum, ink, gold
4 3/4 x 3 1/4
Lent by David and Hazel Stanley

Book of Hours
France, Paris
1497
Antoine Verard, publisher;
Etienne Jehannot, printer
vellum, black ink, metal cut illustrations
7 3/4 x 4 3/4
George A. Smathers Libraries, Special Collections and Area Studies
Z64.02 L3636 1497

Christ on the Cross
Germany
1485
hand-colored woodcut
9 1/3 x 5 1/4
National Gallery of Art, Washington, D.C.
Rosenwald Collection
1943.3.480

The Madonna Between Saints Catherine and Barbara
Germany
1440-1460
hand-colored woodcut
7 1/3 x 5 1/4
National Gallery of Art, Washington, D.C.
Rosenwald Collection
1943.3.570

Book of Hours, Hours of the Virgin
France, Rouen
late 15th century
vellum, ink, tempera, cloth
7 1/8 x 5 1/8
The Pierpont Morgan Library, New York
MS.M.167

Book of Hours, Hours of the Virgin
France, Paris
August, 1542
ink on paper, hand-colored woodcuts
The Pierpont Morgan Library, New York
PML 126044

Pendant with St. Nicholas
Russia
16th century
copper alloy
1 7/8 x 1 5/8
Lent by Gary Hollingsworth, Orlando, Florida

Crucifix
Republic of Congo or Democratic Republic of Congo, Kongo People
17th century
wood, metal
8 1/2 x 5 3/8 x 1
Harn Museum of Art Collection
Museum purchase, funds provided by museum visitors
1998.3

Portable Diptych
Ethiopia
17th century
wood, tempera
3 3/4
Courtesy, Peabody Essex Museum, Salem, MA
E67878

Our Lady of Mercy with St. Peter Nolasco and B. Maria Socorro
Mexico
18th century
paint on copper
10 1/2 x 8
International Folk Art Foundation Collections in the Museum of International Folk Art, a unit of the Museum of New Mexico, Santa Fe
FA.1986.406.1

Thumb Bible
United States, New York City
Printed by S. Wood
1813
1 3/8 x 3/4
paper, black ink, wood-engraved illustrations
George A. Smathers Libraries, Special Collections and Area Studies
23h966

Rafael Aragón
American (c. 1796-1862)
Our Lady of Guadalupe
c. 1830s
wood, polychromy
22 3/4 x 14
Collections of the Museum of International Folk Art, a unit of the Museum of New Mexico, Santa Fe, bequest of Charles D. Carroll
A.1971.31.60

José Benito Ortega
American, New Mexico (1858-1941)
Our Lady of Sorrows
before 1907
wood, polychromy, seeds, wire, aluminum
22 5/8 x 8 5/8 x 5
Harn Museum of Art Collection
Gift of Mr. and Mrs. Thomas J. Needham
1990.8.17

Neck Cross
Russia
18th-19th century
wood
2 x 1 1/2
Lent by Gary Hollingsworth, Orlando, Florida

Icon of the Virgin and Child
Russia
c. 1900
wood, tempera, silver leaf
14 x 13 1/4
Lent by Gary Hollingsworth, Orlando, Florida

St. Anthony
Puerto Rico
probably 19th century
wood, polychromy
11
Spanish Colonial Arts Society, Inc., Collections on loan to the Museum of New Mexico, Museum of International Folk Art, Santa Fe, the Ann and Alan Vedder Collection
PR.68.67.PG

Neck Cross
Ethiopia
19th century
silver
2 1/8 x 1 7/8
Courtesy, Peabody Essex Museum, Salem, MA
E67912

St. Vincent Ferrer
Philippines
probably 19th century
wood, polychromy
21 1/4
International Folk Art Foundation Collections in the Museum of International Folk Art, a unit of the Museum of New Mexico, Santa Fe
FA.1969.28.3

Rosary
Mexico
19th-20th century
gold
30 1/2
International Folk Art Foundation Collections in the Museum of International Folk Art, a unit of the Museum of New Mexico, Santa Fe
FA. 1963.9.47

George T. Lopez
American, New Mexico (1900-1993)
Archangel Rafael
mid-20th century
wood, leather
20 x 16 x 4
Harn Museum of Art Collection
Gift of Mr. and Mrs. Thomas J. Needham
1990.8.18

Palomino Family
Peru, Cuzco
Household Altars
1975
6 3/4 x 4 1/2 x 2
gesso, wood, gold leaf
Harn Museum of Art Collection
Purchase partially made possible by a grant from the U.S. Office of Education
AC-P-75-14 (a & b)

Stephen Antonakos
American, b. 1926, Laconia, Greece
Wall Cross with Votive Candle
1995
wood, glass, wax candle
26 1/2 x 8 x 13
Lent by Stephen Antonakos

José Negrón
Puerto Rican, b. Corozal, 1928
Our Lady of Montserrat Miracle of Hormigueros
1997
wood, polychromy
16 1/2 x 11 5/8 x 8 5/8
Lent from a private collection

ISLAMIC

Folio from a Koran
Turkey
2nd half of 16th century
script: Muhaqqaq and Naskh
paper, opaque watercolor, ink, gold
14 1/4 x 10
Courtesy of the Arthur M. Sackler Gallery, Smithsonian Institution, Washington, D.C.
The Vever Collection
S1986.368b

Book of Prayers
Turkey
August-September 1715
script: Naskh
paper, opaque watercolor, ink, gold
9 1/2 x 16 1/2
Courtesy of the Arthur M. Sackler Gallery, Smithsonian Institution, Washington, D.C.
The Vever Collection
S1986.482

Koran
Turkey
1797
script: Naskh
paper, opaque watercolor, ink, gold
6 1/2 x 4 1/2
George A. Smathers Libraries, Special Collections and Area Studies
Rare Book 1

Crescent Necklace
Somalia
18th century
silver, amber
19
Foundation for Cross-Cultural Understanding, Washington, D.C.

Koranic Amulet
Somalia, Xamar Weyn
18th century
silver, amber, red beads
20
Foundation for Cross-Cultural Understanding, Washington, D.C.

Koranic Amulet
Somalia, Jennali
18th century
silver
23 1/4
Foundation for Cross-Cultural Understanding, Washington, D.C.

Mughal-style Prayer Rug
Northern India
c. 1800
silk and cotton fabric, embroidered with silk thread
45 x 30
Lent from a private collection

Prayer Rug
West Anatolia
c. 1850
wool
59 x 40
Lent by Mr. and Mrs. Jon M. Anderson

Prayer Rug
Iran, Tabriz
1880-1900
cotton and wool
70 x 50
Lent by Mr. and Mrs. Jon M. Anderson

Koran
East Africa, Siyu, Swahili
19th century
locally manufactured inks on northern Italian paper
10 1/4
Fowler Museum of Cultural History, UCLA
Gift of Jerome L. Joss
X90-184a

Prayer Rug
Caucasus, Chechen
late 19th century
wool
76 x 46
Lent from a private collection

Hand of Fatima
Algeria
20th century
gold
1 3/4 x 1
Lent by Dr. Aida A Bamia

Koran Box
Israel, Jerusalem
20th century
wood, mother of pearl
1 1/2 x 6 3/4 x 5
Lent by Dr. Aida A. Bamia

Koran
Nigeria, Kanuri People of Borno State
20th century
ink on paper
9 1/2 x 7 1/4 x 4 1/4
Lent by Professor and Mrs. Ronald Cohen

Prayer Beads
Israel
20th century
mother of pearl
10 1/2
Lent by Dr. Sami Zalatimo

Koranic Board
Nigeria, Hausa People
1966
wood, leather, paper, pigment
21 11/16 x 11 3/4 x 1 1/4
Harn Museum of Art Collection
Museum purchase, funds provided by museum visitors
1997.25

Pitcher
Somalia, Mogadishu
date unknown
silver and alloy
8
Lent by Martin and Evelyn Ganzglass

INTIMATE RITUALS AND PERSONAL DEVOTIONS

Spiritual Art through the Ages

August 12, 2000 to January 14, 2001

Published on the occasion of the first
Samuel P. Harn Memorial Exhibition

Funding for this exhibition and catalogue was generously provided
by a special grant from the AEC Charitable Trust

Special appreciation is extended to the administration of the University of Florida
Charles E. Young, Interim President
David R. Colburn, Interim Provost

Harn Museum exhibitions and programs are sponsored in part by:

The State of Florida, Florida Department of State,
Division of Cultural Affairs and the Florida Arts Council
The Institute of Museum and Library Services
The University of Florida
Harn Museum Program Endowment Fund
The Harn Alliance
The Museum Store and
Private Donations

Accredited by the
American Association of Museums

PRODUCTION CREDITS

Editor: Myra L. Engelhardt
Designer: Meredith Davis
Publication Coordinator: Karen Ilyse Wyman

This catalogue has been set in Matrix and printed on Vintage Velvet in an edition of 4000 copies by Theo Davis Sons, Zebulon, North Carolina

PHOTOGRAPHY CREDITS

Courtesy of Mr. and Mrs. Jon M. Anderson—Plate 13
Courtesy of an anonymous lenders—Plate 14; Figures 36, 37, 39
© 1995 Stephen Antonakos. Photo: Greg Heins—Figure 60
Courtesy of the Arthur M. Sackler Gallery, Smithsonian Institution, Washington, D.C. (S1986.368b, S1986.482)—Figures 58, 59
© Asian Art Museum of San Francisco—Figures 5, 6, 30, 32; Plate 10
Randy A. Battista—Plates 2, 6; Figures 23, 27, 34, 56, 57
© The Cleveland Museum of Art, 1999—Plate 7; Figures 15, 16, 24, 28, 33, 35
© The Cleveland Museum of Art, 2000—Figure 29
© President and Fellows of Harvard College. Harvard University Photographic Services—Figures 14, 25, 31, 40
© President and Fellows of Harvard College. Harvard University. Photo: Michael Nedzweski—Figure 38
© The Jewish Museum, New York, New York. Photo: Richard Goodbody—Plate 3; Figure 8
© The Jewish Museum, New York, New York. Photo: John Parnell—Figure 7
Museum of New Mexico, Museum of International Folk Art, Santa Fe. Photos: Blair Clark—Figures 1, 3
© 2000 Board of Trustees, National Gallery of Art, Washington—Plate 4
Courtesy, Peabody Essex Museum, Salem, MA—Figures 10, 26
The Pierpont Morgan Library, New York, 2000, ms m 167, f. 153. Photography: Joseph Zehavi—Plate 1
Courtesy, Drs. Geoffrey and Ming-mei Redmond—Plate 8
University of Florida, Office of Instructional Resources—Plate 11, 12: Figures 2, 4, 9, 11, 12, 41, 55, 58
Vanderbilt Fine Arts Gallery—Plate 5
© Virginia Museum of Fine Arts. Photo: Ann Hutchison—Plate 9
The Shelby White and Leon Levy Collection. Photographs by Sheldan Collins—Figures 13, 17-22